They will come back, come back again,
As long as the red Earth rolls.
He never wasted a leaf or a tree.
Do you think He would squander souls?
   — Rudyard Kipling

Death & Reincarnation

ETERNITY'S VOYAGE

SRI CHINMOY

Published by
AUM PUBLICATIONS:
86-24 Parsons Blvd., Jamaica, N.Y. 11432

CONTENTS

Preface

The very mention of death instils fear in our hearts. We feel that death is the merciless and inexorable end of our journey on earth, the destroyer of all hopes; but as much as possible we avoid thinking about it altogether. When death strikes in our immediate circle, we are overcome with a sense of permanent loss, and with an intense awareness of our own limitation and mortality.

We cannot escape death, but can we escape the fear of death? In this volume, a fully enlightened spiritual Master teaches us that we *can* overcome the fear of death. How? By understanding the significance of death as a brief respite in the process of our continuous spiritual evolution, which takes place inside the Heart of our Creator. Sri Chinmoy assures us most convincingly of the immortality of the soul, our divine essence, which proceeds dauntlessly toward the goal of illumination through many lifetimes, adopting many forms. Death, he explains, is a mere pause, an opportunity for renewal and reflection for the soul before its next adventure on earth.

The simplicity and immediacy of Sri Chinmoy's words clarify our doubts and assuage our anxieties about death. With equal mastery he describes the progress-march of reincarnation and the unique opportunity of human birth on this supremely chosen planet. Nothing is ever lost; death itself bows to the indomitable soul. This is the powerful message transparently conveyed by a knower of the Unknown.

CHAPTER 1

The Realm of Death

Why is death necessary? Why can't the soul keep on progressing and evolving in the same body?

Right now death is required; death is necessary for us. We cannot do anything for a long time at a stretch. We play for forty-five minutes or an hour and then become tired and have to take rest. It is the same with our aspiration. Suppose we live on the earth for sixty or seventy years. Out of sixty or seventy years we may meditate for twenty days or thirty days and, even then, for only a few hours. An ordinary human being may not aspire in his meditation for even one hour at a stretch. How can he have the aspiration or reality or consciousness that will take him to the eternal Truth or undying Consciousness all at once?

Right now death helps us in a sense; it allows us to take some rest. Then when we come back, we come back with new hope, new light, new aspiration. But if we had a conscious aspiration, a mounting flame burning within us all the time, then we would see that physical death could easily be conquered. A day will dawn when there will be no necessity for death. But right now we do not have that capacity; we are weak. Spiritual Masters, liberated souls, however, do have mastery over death, but they leave the body when the Divine wants them to.

An ordinary man who has shouldered the burden of a whole family for twenty, thirty or forty years will say, "I am tired. Now I need a rest." For him death really has meaning; the soul goes into the soul's region and enjoys a short rest. But for a divine warrior, a seeker of the Ultimate Truth, death has no meaning. He wants to make his progress continuous, without halt. So he will try to live in constant aspiration, eternal aspiration. And with that eternal aspiration, he will try to conquer death so he can be an eternal outer manifestation of the Divine within him.

Is it possible for a man to learn what death is while still living, by actually entering into death?

What death actually is one can easily know when one is in the very highest stage of meditation. Hundreds of times I have experienced what death is. I have also passed beyond death in my meditation many times when I have had to help my disciples. In trance one goes to many worlds, many planes, many regions beyond the domains and boundaries of death.

Sometimes we can actually follow a soul when the soul leaves the body, and then we can get the full experience of death while remaining in the body. I had my first experience of this with one of my sisters, who died when I was eighteen. I had this power, so I followed my sister's soul for about three hours in the world of death. What happens is that you feel that you are actually dead. Your body does not exist for you; only with your consciousness you are flying, flying like a kite. When you have this power, you can have the real experience of death in this world. During your meditation you can easily go. You can keep your body in the world of life and your consciousness-light in the world of death.

Would you explain the spiritual significance of this practice or the need for it?

There is no need for it, but if one wants to learn it in this world, one can easily do so. These things will not help us even an iota in our God-realisation, but if we have time, if we have patience, if we have eagerness, then there is no harm. It is like travelling on a road. We can go directly to the goal or, if we want, we can walk around and look at the scenery or have some fruit from the trees, and while eating the fruit, continue on toward the goal. Everybody in the spiritual life will have the experience of death at least once before self-realisation.

Is death painful?

It depends on the individual. If the individual has not prayed and meditated and has not followed the spiritual life, then it is really painful to part with this life because he does not want to surrender to God's Will. First of all, it is not in him to know or feel what God's Will is. Also, he does not feel God's conscious Protection, Guidance and Concern, so he feels that he is totally lost. In this world he cannot do anything; in the other world all is uncertainty. If there is no aspiration, there is tremendous fear, for ordinary people feel that death is something totally unknown. They do not know where they are going. But seekers know that they are going to the Supreme, to the Lord's Abode. It is temporarily unknown to them, but that consciousness, that plane, is a realm of peace and rest. It belongs to the Supreme, their Eternal Father. So they have no fear.

Then, of course, there is physical pain. At the time of death, even right up to the last moment, if somebody is suffering from a disease and if he cannot throw this disease into something higher or deeper, naturally his last days will be extremely painful. Even the last moment will be very painful because the death-being will come to him in a very destructive form. The death-force, death-being, appears before each individual in a different form according to his soul's achievement and realisation on earth.

Ordinary people who are not aspiring, people who are absolutely wallowing in the pleasures of ignorance, will feel death as a terrible, ruthless being, a dark and awful figure. Sometimes the death-force has many subordinates which come before the dying person, and people very often see tigers or unimaginably huge beings, and become frightened. But sincere seekers see their spiritual Master or a luminous being, like an angel, taking them in a chariot. These seekers have worked hard on earth for many years and now Mother-Earth consciously wants to offer them her blessingful and divine gratitude. Their Inner Pilot or their Guru takes them, but they see the benign Hand of God right in front of them, carrying them in His Golden Boat to the other Shore. Some people see their long-departed relatives at the actual time of death. Their dearest ones come, and it is just like somebody who knows the way taking them to a new world.

When we are caught by the fetters of ignorance, there will be pain both within us and without at the time of our physical death. This pain is due to the ignorance in the human mind and human body which prevents us from entering into the realm of death and then going beyond the realm of death consciously and deliberately. But if the veil of ignorance is removed, then there can be no pain, either in death or in the world-atmosphere. If we can enter into the root of our suffering and pain, which is ignorance, and if we can transform ignorance with our soul's light, then death will be just like a passage leading us to another shore. This other shore is the Light Eternal which guides, protects, shapes and moulds us through Eternity

How can we overcome the fear of death?

Right now you are afraid of death because you think of yourself as your body, your mind, your senses. But a day will come when, on the strength of your aspiration, prayer and meditation, you will think of yourself not as the body but as the soul. You will think of yourself as a conscious instrument of God. Since God is omnipresent, and He is utilising you to manifest Himself, how can He ever abandon you to death?

Conquering the fear of death depends on how much love you have for God and how sincerely you need Him. If you need someone, immediately you establish a kind of inner access to that person. If your need for God is soulful, devoted and constant, then in the inner world you establish a free access to God's Love, God's Compassion, God's Concern. And if you can always feel God's Love, Compassion and Concern, then how can you be afraid of death? The moment you feel that you need God and He needs you, the moment you feel God inside you, before you and around you, then death no longer exists for you. When God is away from your mind, when God is not to be found inside your heart, when you feel that God is nowhere near you, at that time death exists for you. Otherwise, where is death? This physical body may leave the earth, but the soul, which is a conscious portion of God, will remain consciously in God and for God throughout Eternity. It is up to you to think of yourself as the body or as the soul. If you think of yourself as the body and do not aspire, then in the spiritual life you are already dead. But if you think of yourself as the soul, that means you have already developed an inner connection with God. If you know that the soul is your real reality, you will not have any fear of death.

Can meditation help people overcome their fear of death?

Certainly. Meditation can easily help the seeker to overcome the fear of death. Meditation means conscious communication with God. If one can establish his oneness with God, who is all Life, then there can be no fear of death. He will not only conquer fear of death, but he will also conquer something else. He will conquer his doubt about God's existence in his own life or in others' lives. It is very easy for us to feel that God exists only in us, or only in spiritual people. But if we meditate, then it becomes clear to us that God exists not only within us but also inside the people whom we do not like or appreciate.

Why is it that so many linger in pain for a long time before dying?

Many sick people want to die because their pain is unbearable. They want to be free from their suffering.

But why do they still linger and suffer? It is because purification of their nature has not been completed. Through purification we enter into a higher life and a more fulfilling divinity. This is where the law of karma operates. In our past lives, we have done many things wrong. It is through this physical pain that we are purified. This experience is necessary, because through it a new wisdom dawns in the person's consciousness. But when someone suffers bitterly we should not think of his past actions, that he led a bad life and had a bad character, and for this he is suffering. No, let us become one with the experience that he is going through. When we are one with the experience, we get true satisfaction in our human existence.

Again, I have to say that the law of karma is not simple; it is very, very complicated. Some souls are very pure and spiritual, but still they suffer when they die. Is it because of their past wrong karma? No, it is because they identify with humanity and want to experience for themselves the bitterest kind of suffering. Most of the great spiritual Masters have had very painful deaths. Why? At their own sweet will they could have left their body, but they did not do it. Instead they contracted cancer and other serious diseases, and only after much suffering did they die. In their case, what they were doing was entering into humanity's suffering and trying to feel how humanity suffers. Unless we enter into the suffering of humanity, everything is theoretical; nothing is practical. But if ordinary people suffer, we see that it is the law of karma that is operating.

Nevertheless, if someone dies of sudden heart failure, that does not necessarily mean that he was very spiritual or religious. No, God wanted to have this particular experience through him, and perhaps through his loved ones, at that particular time. Here there is no question of good or bad, divine or undivine, but of what kind of experience God wanted to have in that particular person. Ultimately everything is an experience of God that we are seeing or having.

Is it possible for a spiritual person who is dying a painful death to transform his pain into joy through meditation?

If one is a sincere seeker, then even while he is dying, great joy will come. Although the physical may suffer, the delight of the soul will come forward, enabling one to meditate consciously. Sometimes, when one consciously enters into the pain, then one's own inner courage in the pain itself is transformed into joy.

One can consciously enter into pain even while undergoing a serious operation. When I was a young boy, eighteen or nineteen years old, I did this during a serious operation. While the doctor was operating on me I consciously entered into the pain and felt real joy. I was smiling at the doctor, and he simply could not understand it. This anybody can experience.

In one of the daily meditations in your book you mention that death is an obstruction. I always thought you considered death to be a transition that just enables us to be reborn and make continuing progress.

I have said that death is a transition. I have said that life and death are like two rooms: life is my living room, and death is my bedroom. When I say that death is an obstruction, I am speaking of death from a different point of view. What is an obstruction? An obstruction is something that prevents us from going farther. It is a limit which we cannot go beyond.

This life is a golden opportunity given to us by the Supreme. Now opportunity is one thing and achievement is another. Our spiritual evolution, our inner progress is very steady, very slow and, at the same time, most significant. Naturally there are people who for hundreds or thousands of incarnations will follow a normal, natural cycle of birth and death. Then one day, in God's Eternity, they will realise God. But some sincere, genuine aspirants make a soulful promise that in this incarnation, here and now, they shall realise God. They say this in spite of knowing that this is not their first life or their last life. They know that there are people who have realised God and they do not want to wait for some distant future incarnation. They feel that it is useless to live without God-realisation and they want to have it as soon as possible.

In such cases, if death comes and they are still unrealised, then death is an obstruction. If somebody who is destined to die at the age of fifty is aspiring soulfully, if he can push his death back, with the kindest approval of the Supreme, for another twenty or thirty years, then during this period what will he be doing? He will be continuing his sincere aspiration, his deepest meditation, his highest contemplation. He will be like a racer running towards his Goal with no obstruction. During these extra twenty or thirty years he may reach the farthest end, where his Goal lies.

But if death interferes, then he does not realise God in this life. In the following incarnation very few souls can immediately take up the thread of their past aspiration. As soon as one enters into the world, the undivine cosmic forces come and attack, and the ignorance, limitations and imperfections of the world try to cover the soul. In the formative years of childhood, one does not remember anything. A child is innocent, ignorant and helpless. Then, after a few years, the mind starts functioning. When one is between eight and twelve years old, the mind complicates everything. So for the first eleven, twelve or thirteen years of the next incarnation almost all souls, despite being very great and spiritual, forget their past achievements and deepest inner cry.

Now there are spiritual Masters or great seekers who get a few high experiences in their childhood or who start thinking and singing about God at a very early age, but usually there is no strong connecting link between the soul's achievement on earth in its previous incarnation and these childhood years in the present incarnation. There is a link, a very subtle link, but this link does not function significantly for the first twelve or thirteen years.

Some souls do not regain the aspiration of their past incarnation until the age of fifty or sixty. From the spiritual point of view, these fifty or sixty years in their following incarnation are absolutely wasted time. So in this incarnation if one loses fifty years, and if in the past incarnation one has lost twenty or thirty years, then it is eighty years wasted. In this case I say that death is a real obstruction. We have to remove that obstruction with our aspiration, our unbroken aspiration. Aspiration should be like a bullet. It should pass through the death wall.

But even though it may take some time, eventually the inner being will come consciously to the fore and the person in his new incarnation will start praying and meditating on God most powerfully and sincerely. At that time he will see that nothing from his past has really been lost. Everything has been saved up in the earth-consciousness, which is the common bank for everyone. The soul will know how much it has achieved on earth; and all this is kept very safely inside the earth-consciousness, the earth-bank. You deposit money here in the bank. Then you can go to England and after six years or more you can come back and take out your money. The soul does the same thing after having left the earth for ten or twenty years. All the soul's achievements are kept here intact in Mother-Earth. Then Mother-Earth gives them back again when the soul returns to work for God on earth.

Nothing is lost except time, in most cases, during those few years of childhood. But it is better to realise God in one incarnation so that we do not lose our conscious aspiration again in this transitory period. If we can continue on earth for fifty to one hundred years with tremendous, sincere aspiration, then we can accomplish much. If we get help from a real spiritual Master, it is possible to realise God in one incarnation, or in two or three. If there is no real Master and if there is no aspiration, it takes hundreds and hundreds of incarnations.

When we die, what is the best thing to do?

For a spiritual person, the best thing to do is to remember the presence of his Master. The near and dear ones should place a picture of his spiritual guide right in front of the seeker, and let the Master be with him spiritually when the seeker breathes his last. Let the Master be inside the very breath, the very last breath of the seeker. Then it is the duty, the responsibility of the inner guide to do what is necessary. Long before you leave the body your Master will have left the body. So you can meditate on me and I will help you.

Last year your father died. If you had been physically present, what you should have done at that time was to meditate most soulfully. Although your father was not consciously my disciple and had not accepted our path, who knows what he will do in his next incarnation? You knew that there was somebody who could have helped your father while he was dying, so you should have meditated on me. One always knows who can help in any situation. When somebody is sick, one calls the doctor. When somebody is in legal trouble, one gets the help of a lawyer. If you had wanted to help your father, immediately you should have thought of me and meditated on me. If you had had tremendous aspiration or spiritual power, you would have given him all your spiritual strength. But your spiritual strength right now is your aspiration, and the source of your aspiration is inside this Master, your Guru. So if you want to help your dearest ones, you have to do it in this way.

But if you are speaking of other people, then in order to know what is best to do when they are dying, you have to know who gave them the greatest joy on earth, or in whom they had their greatest faith. If somebody had all faith in Christ, even though you may not follow the path of Christ, immediately you have to consciously and most devotedly invoke the presence of Christ. You have to help your friend at that time to increase his faith in Christ. You can repeat the name of Christ out loud, and bring him a picture of Christ and read from the

Bible. In this way you will be able to help his aspiration. If somebody spiritual who knows me is dying, at that time you should read my writings and speak about me. But if it is someone who is just an acquaintance, you should increase his faith in his own way.

Is there any special way we should meditate on a person who is dying?

Suppose you have gone to see a casual acquaintance in the hospital. At that time you should concentrate on his heart. You do not have to look at the person, but put your whole concentration on his heart.

First try to imagine a circle at his heart, and then try to feel that this circle is rotating there like a disc. That means that life-energy is now revolving consciously in the aspiration or in the vessel of the person who is sick. Through your concentration and meditation, you are entering into the heartbeat of that person. When you enter into the heartbeat, then your consciousness and the aspiring or dying consciousness of the other person rotate together. While they are rotating, pray with your whole being to the Supreme, who is your Guru and everybody's Guru, "Let Thy Victory be achieved. Let Thy Will be done through this particular individual. I want only Your Victory." Victory does not necessarily mean that the person will be cured. No, God may have decided that this person must leave the body for a very good reason. If you pray to God in a surrendered way and if the person leaves the body, then you are fulfilling God and you are fighting for the Victory of God. If God wants to take him to Heaven to do something for Him there, then naturally it is God's Victory when the person leaves the body. If you pray for the Supreme's Victory, with your aspiration you are giving all the responsibility to the Supreme. When you can consciously give the responsibility to the Supreme, you are doing the right thing.

What should be the attitude of the dear ones when somebody close is dying?

We are all like passengers on a single train. The destination has come for one particular passenger. He has to get off at this stop, but we still have to go on and cover more distance. Now we have to know that this hour of death has been sanctioned by the Supreme. Without the approval or tolerance of the Supreme, no human being can die. So if we have faith in the Supreme, if we have love and devotion for the Supreme, we will feel that the Supreme is infinitely more compassionate than any human being, infinitely more compassionate than we who want to keep our dear ones. Even if the dying person is our son, or our mother or father, we have to know that he is infinitely dearer to the Supreme than he is to us. The Supreme is our Father and our Mother. If one member of the family goes to the father and mother, the other members of the same family will never feel sad.

If we have taken to the spiritual life and want to have real joy, we must know that we can have this joy only by surrendering our life to the Will of the Supreme. Now we may not know what the Will of the Supreme is, but we do know what surrender is. If the Supreme wants to take somebody away from our life, we must accept this. "Let Thy Will be done." If this is our attitude, then we will have the greatest joy. And this joy does the greatest service to the one who is going to depart. When we totally surrender to the Supreme, this surrender becomes additional strength and power for the departing soul that is suffering here in bondage. So if we really surrender our will to the Will of the Supreme, then this surrender will verily bring peace, an abiding peace, to the soul that is about to leave the earth-scene.

Those who have started meditating and concentrating are getting glimpses of their past incarnations. If we believe we had a past and we know we have a present, then we can also feel that we will have a future. Knowing this, we have to be always conscious of this truth: that there is no death. In the Bhagavad Gita it is said, "As a man discards his old clothes and puts on new ones, so does the soul discard this physical body and take on a new body." When we know that the person who is going to die is just leaving aside this old body before accepting a new one, and if the person who is dying also has the same knowledge, how can there be any fear?

We do not know what death actually is; that is why we want to stay here on earth as long as possible. But real death is not the dissolution of the physical body. Real death, spiritual death, is something else.

I had a young friend who died just six weeks ago. The day before he died he told his father that he would die the next day, and then he did. How could he know?

Why not? Is he not God's child? At the time of death, if one thinks of God all the time, one may get the message from one's own inner being. When my own mother was passing away, I happened to be at my uncle's house, six miles away. My mother was suffering from goiter. Early in the morning she said, "This morning I am leaving the body. Where has Madal gone? Send for him." Then a cousin of mine brought me the message and I came. She took my hand, then gave me a smile, her last smile. She left about a minute after I arrived, as if she had waited for me. Now I must be truthful. My mother was very, very spiritual, and used to practise the inner life in the strictest sense of the term. But about your friend, I must say that hundreds and thousands of people have known in advance when they were going to die. And for spiritual people it is very easy. They often know a few months in advance.

Is it written in a person's palm when he will die?

From the palm you cannot always tell when someone will die. If it is an accidental death, the palm may not be correct, but the forehead is always correct. It gives an immediate vibration. The forehead will have written on it what will happen to the individual tomorrow, and it will be visible on the nose if there is going to be an accidental death.

I once had a friend who was very fond of me. His name was Ravi. One day he was practising javelin at six o'clock in the evening. When I took the javelin from him I saw death forces in him. I thought, "Best thing is to forget about it, or pray to God." I didn't want to know about it. The following day, I was going down some stairs, and he was near the staircase. There I saw the same force and I cursed myself, saying it was all my mental hallucination. An hour and a half later, I heard that he had had an accident. He was riding a motor bike behind a truck with his friend. They were following the truck. The truck lowered its speed, and this fellow thought he also was lowering his speed, but he pressed the handle the wrong way and increased the speed, so he dashed against the truck. The truck driver heard the sound. He took both of them to the hospital. They were put in one room. Ravi's mother came to see him, but she was not allowed in because the doctor said that both the cases were serious. I think he lived only for three hours. So an apparition came to me while I was practising javelin. The day he died was the day of our javelin competition, but I did not go there; I only went to the funeral. In his case it was destined that he die.

When a person is sick and, medically speaking, there is no hope of recovery, is it good to tell the person he is going to die and to start helping him get ready for departure?

This is a very complicated question; each case has to be considered separately. Most people want to live; they do not want to die because they do not know what death is. They think that death is a tyrant who will torture them in every way and finally destroy them. When somebody's karma is over and the Supreme wants that particular person to leave the body, if the person has vital hunger and unsatisfied desires—even though the soul does not have these desires—then the person wants to stay on earth. He does not want to obey the Will of the Supreme. So what should you do when a person has this kind of standard? If you tell him that God does not want him to stay on earth anymore, that he has had all the necessary experiences in this body, then he will misunderstand. He will say: "God does not want me to leave the body; it is you who want this." He will think you are cruel and merciless. So if you know that it is the Will of the Supreme that this particular person should leave the world, the best thing is to silently speak to the soul of the person and try to inspire him to abide by the Will of God.

But if the person is very spiritual and a sincere seeker, then he himself will say to his relatives and dear ones: "Pray to God to take me away. I have finished my play here on earth. Read me spiritual books—the scriptures, the Bible, the Gita. Let me hear only divine things, spiritual things, which will help me start out on my journey." There are many, many people in India who, when they feel that their days are numbered, say: "The sooner He takes me, the better." When my mother was dying, she read the Gita constantly during her last few days with the attitude, "Now I am going to the Eternal Father. Let me prepare myself." A patient of that type receives greater joy in knowing and obeying the Will of the Supreme.

Is it always best for doctors to keep people alive as long as possible, or does it depend on the individual case?

If a person is spiritual, the doctors and relatives should always try to keep him on earth as long as possible, because spiritual people are always fighting against death. But it may happen that somebody who is absolutely useless is going to die in two hours. Even if you keep him on earth for twenty-four hours more, he is not going to utter God's name even once. But if somebody has the capacity to utter God's name soulfully just once more during his life, then he will achieve something in the soul's world. That achievement will be added to the other achievements of this life and in his next incarnation his life will be a little bit better.

In India some people live for over two hundred years, but they do not have time to pray to God even once in six months or a year. From a spiritual point of view, these people are like a solid piece of stone. For them each additional year is just another waste of time. But if one can stay on earth even one hour more and invoke the presence of the Supreme during that hour, then naturally it is better for that person to stay on earth. Even unconsciously if someone is thinking of God, then it is better for him to stay as long as possible on earth.

If the doctors kill a patient who is supposed to remain alive, will they get bad karma?

When doctors consciously do something wrong, they create wonderful problems for their future incarnations. Doctors are not perfect; they may not know enough about medical science. If they make a mistake and accidentally kill a patient, their ignorance is forgiven by the Supreme. Again, if they cannot pay sufficient attention because they have too many patients, the Supreme sees whether or not it is their fault. But if they deliberately kill someone just to get rid of the patient, then the law of karma is there to take care of them.

There is a girl who has been totally unconscious for weeks. They say she can live for years with no consciousness. What about a case like that?

If there is even the least hope that the life-force is operating in and through the person, the best thing is to try to keep her on earth. As long as the soul is in the body, then there is hope for the person. For five months if the person stays on earth, there is some purpose.

*They're not trying to bring her back to conscious-
ness; they're just keeping her body alive. They say
her brain is not functioning at all. There are no
brain waves.*

They should continue because the life-energy is still
operating. If the soul is not there, the machine cannot
keep the body alive for more than a few hours. When
the vibration of the soul remains, even if somebody has
left the house, you will feel his lingering presence.
Similarly, the heart keeps pumping because the vibration of the soul still remains.

Is there any reason for this kind of experience?

The Supreme is using His law of karma. Suppose the
parents have done something seriously wrong to this girl
in a previous incarnation. Now the soul says, "All right,
in this incarnation I am going to purify you. I will linger
and linger and linger. You will have to pay the penalty
for your wrong action. In this incarnation I am taking
revenge." If the soul knows that the patient is not going
to be cured, and if the family members know, then at
that time it is revenge.

Either the soul is enjoying the experience, or it is
waiting for the right moment to leave, or it is just having
an experience. We feel that the person is really dead,
but who knows what kind of experience the soul is having? Instead of five minutes, this can go on for five
years. Anything is possible. Again, it may not be a
healthy experience, but the soul wants to go through it.
Ordinary human beings often do something for many
years just to show the world that it is possible, but that
very thing need not be encouraging or inspiring.

Can you postpone with your will-power the time of death?

Certainly.

Can you postpone it indefinitely?

Spiritual Masters can postpone it indefinitely if it is God's Will. A spiritual person gets this power when he has attained to spiritual perfection, because then he is absolutely surrendered to God. A disciple comes to a Guru and surrenders entirely to him. Similarly, a Guru has to make absolute surrender to God the Infinite. In this surrender he becomes one with God. He does not break the Law of God; he only tries to fulfil it. If God says, "I want you to leave the body now," he leaves the body. But if he sees that some hostile forces are attacking him and are untimely causing his death, then he uses his power because God wants him to live on earth to help humanity.

Having this power is of no use if you just want to stay on earth for two or three hundred years to live an ordinary animal life. A turtle lives for hundreds of years, but that does not mean that it is better than a human being. What we need is direct illumination, the knowledge of Truth, the knowledge of Light and the knowledge of God. It is not the years, but the achievements, that count.

Have you ever had to actually fight the death-forces to save somebody's life?

Just this last Sunday I came very late to morning meditation because I was fighting with three death-forces that wanted to snatch away three of my close disciples.

With two I was really successful, but with the third I was not at all certain what was going to happen. It wasn't until the following day that I got the assurance that the third one would also survive. Otherwise, that night you would have seen someone in the New York Centre snatched away. He was going to have a heart attack. And the funniest part of the story is that this person was there at the morning meditation, meditating while I was fighting with the death-forces.

I work in a cancer hospital where people frequently die. Sometimes when people are dying I see a quality or a look on their face which is very similar to something that I see in your face. Can you tell me why?

When I am united with the Universal Consciousness, I am in everybody. There are many people on earth who are not my disciples, but they are sincere seekers. God-realised souls who are of the first class will see when sincere seekers pray to God at the time of their death, or when their days are numbered. I tell you, if they pray to God or Christ or anybody, if they are really sincerely knocking at God's door, they can find shining there my face, Buddha's face, Krishna's face because of our Universal Consciousness. Who these people are, I cannot tell. There are hundreds and thousands who are not my direct disciples. But they knock at the Universal Consciousness, and there receive my light, my compassion. That is why you see my face on their face. They see me, and get help from my compassionate inner being. At that time, an illumined part of my being, of my inner existence, goes there to give them some consolation, some little illumination, so that in the soul's world they can have a better existence and can come back again to aspire. If you look at a dying person and if you see my face, then you will know that this person is a seeker. There is no need for him to be my disciple. But if he has extremely sincere aspiration, because of my Universal Consciousness, I can be there.

There are times when my disciples meditate most soulfully on me and identify themselves with me to such an extent that other disciples will see on them my face. Their power of concentration on me is so sincere, so devoted, so one-pointed and soulful, that right on their face the disciples will see my face, even if the person is a woman. This has happened several times.

Sometimes people burn themselves to death as a protest against war. From the spiritual point of view, what does this accomplish?

In a family very often the brothers will fight. Then the mother says, "If you don't stop, I am going to commit suicide." I know of many cases where the parents have committed suicide when they found it impossible to keep harmony in the family. Then the children immediately changed. When they saw that their parents died on account of their fighting, they turned over a new leaf. But this did not last, and soon they were fighting once again.

Now from the spiritual point of view, suicide does not serve any purpose. The mother has sacrificed herself for her children. By her own physical sacrifice she thought that she would create harmony, but in the vital world there is no escape, no forgiveness for her. To the vital world she will go for her stupidity, and there she will stay. Why did she not have the wisdom to see that the children are not her children but God's children? God gave her these children, so why did she not approach God to illumine their consciousness? Why did she not pray to God for their harmony and peace?

The world will remain ignorant unless and until the Supreme illumines the world consciousness. If we sacrifice our individual lives in order to bring about peace, the world's problems will never be solved.

Many martyrs, aspirants and spiritual figures have killed themselves, but it did not solve the problems of the world. These problems will be solved only by aspiration, by praying to God to illumine the world while we are here on earth. Our individual death can never transform the face of the world. But if we invoke God's Blessing, God's Grace and God's Concern, then the problem can be solved.

What is the difference between cremation and a regular burial?

The outer difference you know: when it is cremation the body is burned; when it is burial the body is put into a coffin and buried. Indians especially are fire worshippers. They feel that fire not only consumes everything but also purifies everything. So for fire we have a god, whose name is Agni. We pray to Agni for purification and for self-knowledge, and we also give our dead to him.

From the spiritual point of view, we know that the body has come into existence from five elements: earth, water, air, ether and energy. From five elements the physical sheath came into existence, and with the help of fire it will go back into the five elements. With cremation the physical body will dissolve with utmost purification, which here means transformation.

Again, those in the West who prefer burial also have their own spiritual interpretation. A kind of spiritual compassion comes because the body has served us so faithfully, and we say: "Oh, I utilised this body for so many years and never gave it any rest. Now the soul is not there; the bird has flown away. Let me give the body a chance to rest and have it put into a coffin." Those who care for burning the body feel that the body, which has done so many silly, evil things in this life, needs purification. And those who care for burial want to give the body a comfortable rest.

How does giving your body to science affect you spiritually?

It is neither noble nor ignoble. It is only an individual choice. As you know, sometimes the body is cremated and sometimes it is buried. Once the soul leaves the body, the soul does not care what happens to the body. Once the bird flies away, only the cage remains. At that time we can do anything we want with the cage.

One individual gets satisfaction by saying, "After I die I want to give my body to a hospital so that medical science can make some experiments which will be of great help in the future." But another person says, "Only let God's Will operate in and through my relatives. Let my relatives bury me if they want to; if they want to cremate me, let them cremate me." So he leaves it entirely up to the wishes of the relatives. Or an individual may say, "No, I want tradition to be carried on. I want my body to be buried or cremated in the normal way." But no particular way will necessarily please God more. God has given us the freedom to make an individual choice. If we want cremation, God will say, "Wonderful!" If we want burial, God will say, "Wonderful!" If we want our body to be taken to a hospital for experimentation after the soul leaves, God will in no way be displeased or dissatisfied with us.

You have spoken about physical death. Could you say something about the kind of death and rebirth that occurs in the spiritual life?

When we wholeheartedly, sincerely and unreservedly accept the spiritual life, we feel that it is the real death of ignorance, of desire, of limitation. It is the death of our limited, strangling, unfulfilled and obscure consciousness in the vital. It is the vital that is craving to fulfil all kinds of desires, not the physical, so this death takes place in the vital plane. When we really launch into the spiritual life we have an inner death. This death is the death of our past, of the way we have formed our past.

We will build the edifice of Truth on aspiration, not on desires and worries or anxieties and doubts. The past wanted to show us the Truth in one way. But the past was not able to show us the Truth; that is why we are what we are in the present. Whether the present will show us the Truth or not, we do not know. But we think we will see the Reality either in the immediate present or in the fast-dawning future, the future that is growing in the immediacy of today.

One of the mysteries in the spiritual life is that at every moment we are dying and renewing ourselves. Each moment we see that a new consciousness, a new thought, a new hope, a new light is dawning in us. When something new dawns, at that time we see that the old has been transformed into something higher, deeper and more profound. So in the higher spiritual life, at every moment we can see the so-called death of our limited consciousness and its transformation into a newer, brighter consciousness.

I was actually thinking more in terms of rebirth. How can I become like a child again and accomplish this spiritual rebirth?

This rebirth must take place in the mind, in the body and in the vital. It must take place in the innermost, unconscious part of yourself, that part which was engulfed by ignorance, imperfection and limitation. When this spiritual rebirth takes place and you feel the dawn of a new consciousness in yourself, please try to become that consciousness and give it to your Master and to the Supreme, as you would offer a flower. When you are giving the flower, feel that it is not something you have plucked from a tree, but that it is your entire being which you are placing at the Feet of the Supreme. Then you will see this flower blooming petal by petal, and you will bloom inwardly with your inner fragrance, like a child. Deep within yourself a child will be growing and your outer age will disappear from you. But this will happen only when your aspiring consciousness has full mastery over your body, vital, mind and heart and has made your whole existence into a flower which you have offered at the Feet of the Supreme.

It is inevitable for each human being who has entered into the spiritual life to have a spiritual rebirth in this life. Everyone must feel that he is a conscious, dynamic instrument, a child of the Divine. Everyone has to feel this truth and become this truth. When it is done, the child is no longer a child; he becomes Divinity itself. And then God-realisation is not only possible but inevitable. Only a child has the right to be in the lap of the Father, and the Father is eager to have the child in His lap. He is proud of having the child and the child is proud of having the Father.

Can you say something about Eternity and the Eternal Life?

Being a spiritual man, I can say on the strength of my own inner realisation that the soul does not die. We know that we are eternal. We have come from God, we are in God, we are growing into God and we are going to fulfil God. Life and death are like two rooms; going from life to death is like going from one room to the other. Where I am now is my living room. Here I am talking to you, meditating with you, looking at you. Here I have to show my physical body; I have to work and be active and show my life. Then there is another room, my bedroom. There I take rest; I sleep. There I do not have to show my existence to anybody; I am only for myself.

We come from the Infinite Life, the Life Divine. This Infinite Life stays on earth for a short span of time, say fifty or sixty years. At that time we have within us the earthbound life. But inside this earth-bound life is the boundless Life. After a while this Life again passes through the corridor of death for five or ten or fifteen or twenty years. When we enter this corridor, the soul leaves the body for a short or long rest and goes back to the soul's region. Here, if the person was spiritual, the soul will regain the Eternal Life, the Life Divine which existed before birth, which exists between birth and death, which exists in death and, at the same time, goes beyond death.

Now while we are living on earth, we can place ourselves in the realm of Eternal Life through our aspiration and meditation. But just by entering into the endless Life, we do not possess that Life; we have to grow into it consciously. When we enter into the life of meditation, we must eventually become part and parcel of meditation. And when we are able to meditate twenty-four hours a day we are constantly breathing in the endless Life. In our inner consciousness we have become one with the soul. When we live in the body, there is death all the time. As soon as fear comes into our mind, immediately we die. As soon as some negative forces come, we die. How many times each day we die! Fear, doubt and anxiety are constantly killing our inner existence. But when we live in the soul, there is no such thing as death. There is just a constant evolution of our consciousness, our aspiring life.

CHAPTER 2

Is Death the End?

On 9 November 1970, during his first European lecture tour, Sri Chinmoy delivered the following lecture at the University of Kent, Canterbury, England.

Death is not the end. Death can never be the end. Death is the road. Life is the traveller. The soul is the guide. When the traveller is tired and exhausted, the guide instructs the traveller to take either a short or a long rest, and then the traveller's journey begins again.

In the ordinary life, when an unaspiring man wallows in the mire of ignorance, it is the real victory of death. In the spiritual life, when an aspirant does not cry for a higher light, bliss and power, it is the birth of his death.

What can we learn from the inner life, the life which desires the extinction of death? The inner life tells us that life is soulfully precious, that time is fruitfully precious. Life without the aspiration of time is meaningless. Time without the aspiration of life is useless.

Our mind thinks of death. Our heart thinks of life. Our soul thinks of Immortality. Mind and death can be transcended. Heart and life can be expanded. Soul and Immortality can be fulfilled.

When the mind and death are transcended, man will have a new home: Light, the Light of the Beyond.

When the soul and Immortality are fulfilled, man will have a new goal: Delight, the transcendental Delight.

Today man feels that death is an unavoidable necessity. Tomorrow man will feel that Immortality is an unmistakable reality.

Unfortunately, most of us cherish wrong conceptions about death. We think death is something unusual, something destructive. But we have to know that right now death is something natural, normal and, to some extent, inevitable. Lord Krishna tells Arjuna: "O Arjuna, certain is death for the born and certain is birth for the dead. Therefore what is inevitable ought not to be a cause for thy sorrow."

The Chandogya Upanishad tells us something significant: "When the hour of death approaches, what should we do? We should take refuge in three sublime thoughts: we are indestructible; we can never be shaken; we are the very essence of life." When the hour of death approaches us, if we feel that we can never be destroyed, that nothing can shake us and that we are the very essence of life, then where is sorrow, where is fear, where is death? No death.

Sarada Devi, the consort of Sri Ramakrishna, said something very significant: "The difference between a spiritual man and an ordinary man is very simple. Easily you can know the difference between the two. An ordinary man cries and sheds bitter tears when death approaches him; whereas a spiritual man, if he is really spiritual, will laugh and laugh when death approaches, for to him death is fun, nothing else."

Here we have to say that a spiritual man enters into the Cosmic Game; he becomes a conscious instrument of the Cosmic Game. That is why he knows that death is not an extinction. It is only a short or long rest.

Again and again we shall have to come back into the world. We have to work for God here on earth. There is no escape. We have to realise the Highest here on earth. We have to fulfil the Highest on earth. God will not allow us to waste or squander the potentialities and possibilities of the soul. Impossible.

Kipling's immortal utterance runs:

They will come back, come back again,
As long as the red Earth rolls.
He never wasted a leaf or a tree.
Do you think He would squander souls?

Each incarnation is leading us toward a higher life, a better life. We are in the process of evolution. Each incarnation is a rung in the ladder of evolution. Man is progressing consciously and unconsciously. But if he makes progress in each incarnation consciously, then he is expediting his spiritual evolution. Realisation will take place much sooner for him than for those who are making progress unconsciously.

We know that we started our journey from the mineral life and then entered into the plant life. Then we entered into the animal kingdom. From there we have come into the human world. But this is not the end. We have to grow into divine beings. Unless and until we have become divinised and transformed, God will not be satisfied with us. He can manifest in us and through us only when we are totally transformed and fully illumined. So when we think of our evolution—inner evolution and outer evolution—we should get abundant joy. We lose nothing in so-called death.

Jalalu'd-din Rumi most beautifully and soulfully tells us about evolution:

> A stone I died and rose again a plant;
> A plant I died and rose an animal;
> I died an animal and was born a man.
> Why should I fear? What have I lost by death?

What is death, after all? Death is a sleeping child. And what is life? Life is a child that is playing, singing and dancing at every moment before the Father. Death is the sleeping child inside the Heart of the Inner Pilot. Life is inspiration. Life is aspiration. Life is realisation. Life is not the reasoning mind. Life is not the intellectual mind. Life is not a game of frustration. No, life is the message of divinity on earth. Life is God's conscious channel to fulfil divinity in humanity on earth.

There is much truth in Confucius' saying: "We do not know life. How can we know death?" But I wish to say that we can know life. If we realise life as God's embodiment of truth, light, peace and bliss, then we know what life truly is and recognise death as nothing but a rest—one necessary at the present stage of evolution.

There will come a time when rest will not be necessary at all. Only Life will reign supreme—the Life of the ever-transcending Beyond. This Life is not and cannot be the sole monopoly of an individual. Each human being has to be flooded with this Life of the ever-transcending Beyond, for it is here in this Life Divine that God will manifest Himself unreservedly on earth.

CHAPTER 3

The Realm of Death

In the autumn of 1968, one of Sri Chinmoy's disciples, Virgil Gant, died. The following is an impromptu talk Sri Chinmoy gave at the New York Centre shortly after this disciple's death.

I wish to say a few things about Buddy's [Virgil's] passing. The day he left the physical body, his small nephews asked me, "Where is our Uncle Buddy?" I said, "He is now in Heaven with God." Then they asked, "Can we also go there?" I said, "Certainly you can go, but only when your Father, your Eternal Father, invites you. When your physical father asks you to come to him, you go running; but when he is in some other room and he does not call, you do not go. Similarly, when God, the Eternal Father, calls a particular son of His, the son goes."

Then they said, "Why can't we go there?" I said, "You cannot go there because that place is very, very, very far away, and you need a kind of ticket. Here when you want to go from one place to another you buy a ticket and you go there. For that place there is a special ticket and special money, so when you get these you can go to that place." Then they asked, "Is he thinking of us?" I said, "He is thinking of you constantly. He is thinking of you and blessing you, and his soul will be helping and guiding you."

The day Buddy got his fatal attack, his mother, Karuna, phoned me in the small hours of the morning. I concentrated on him and the moment I did so, I found that his death was just minutes away. Then immediately I went into my highest transcendental consciousness and invoked the Supreme and the Supreme's descending Grace. Later that evening, around six o'clock, the critical period would pass and he would be saved. At that particular hour I saw his soul enter into my room while I was meditating. He said, "Save me, save me." I said, "You are already saved. The Supreme has saved you."

You may say, "He was saved at that time, so how is it that now, a month later, he has left the body?" My answer is this: there is a cosmic Plan, and God has the right to change this cosmic Plan according to His own Will. At first Buddy's soul, with an adamantine will, was fighting to stay on earth, and we identified with his soul. With our prayer, with our concentration, with the force we put on the physical, with our soul's cry, he did stay on earth. But his soul saw that after he was cured this physical body of his would not be able to fulfil the high mission that he was placing in front of himself. When his soul brought forward this high, higher, highest vision right in front of his nose, at first his body was afraid to embrace the vision and reality. But the soul convinced the body that not with this body, but with another form, another body, he would fulfil himself, he would fulfil God and he would fulfil humanity. At 10:15 that morning the Supreme and his soul made the decision that he would leave the body. Immediately afterwards I entered into the occult world and garlanded him with my soul's concern and blessing and all my love and sweetness. About an hour later his soul actually did fly away from the cage.

Now two or three days earlier his mother felt that Buddy was saying good-bye. She felt it because her body, mind, heart and soul were totally one with her child. The decision took place at exactly 10:15 in the morning, but the mother's heart saw the truth before the truth even came into existence. Because of her psychic oneness with Buddy, her intuitive feeling made her know even before God made the decision.

If I act like an ordinary human being who does not identify himself with the Supreme's Will, then from the very depth of my heart I am prepared to say that it was a terrible defeat that Buddy passed away. We lost in the battlefield of life, where each second is an opportunity for the soul to achieve, to materialise, to manifest here on earth. Because I identified with him, I cried and cried from the very depth of my heart. Believe me, I personally can be in my highest and again I can be in my lowest. When I am in the physical I suffer. The first thing I said was, "It is my defeat, my defeat, because I put so much concentration, so much force on him." But from the spiritual point of view, this loss, this defeat, was no defeat. When we are identified with the Will of the Supreme, we feel that His Will is all Compassion and all Fulfilment. The moment we all surrendered to the Will of the Supreme, Buddy left the physical. His mother, his sister, he and I all entered into the Will of the Supreme and said: "Let Thy Will be done."

Now why is it that in the beginning we do not surrender to the Will of the Supreme? First of all, in this world we are identified with the physical. We try to possess our dearest one as long as we can. And secondly, we feel that it may be God's Will that he live in order that his soul may get more inner experiences in the field of manifestation. But our highest Self is always one with the Supreme, and from there we see the eternal Vision and the eternal Reality. When we are one with the Supreme, we feel Eternity as our very own. Buddy was on earth for forty-two years, but his spiritual name, Asim, means eternal, boundless, infinite Life. It is the infinite Life that the soul possesses and cherishes.

When I saw Buddy in the hospital before he died, he said, "Help me get out of the hospital alive." I told him certainly he would be all right. It was not my false compassion, but my genuine feeling, and that feeling was my vision. God is all Love; God is all Wisdom. And although God's decision is ultimate, God can change His Will and make another decision. Later, about three hours after he left the body, he said to me, "I am more alive than ever."

What is the meaning of 'alive' here? To ordinary people, to those who do not believe in God, it is absurd. They will mock me. But those who have entered into the inner life will feel that Buddy is now living in eternal Life. Formerly he was in earthbound life for forty-two years. In these forty-two years he had many, many experiences. But in comparison to the experiences he is having now in one fleeting second, these earthly experiences are nothing. In one fleeting second he is having thousands and millions of experiences in the inner world, and these experiences are the kind that fulfil us within and without.

When Buddy died, the soul of my physical mother came down from the soul's world and took his soul into the vital world. Then my closest friend, my best admirer, my spiritual brother Jyotish, who passed away three years ago, came and took Buddy into a very high world to rest. I went there to see him. He is very happy. I sat beside him and what did he say? He said his physical body was junk. "Did you want me to stay with that body?" And what was I to tell him? "Junk!" he said. That was his word. He wanted me to stay with him for a while and he made me sit. Then we had all kinds of divine jokes, and he told me quite a few secrets, which I have told to the members of his family. I can say a few things about his concern for his dear ones, but the deepest secrets I cannot tell. He said the children must eat more for the next three months. Then last night he came to me and said, "Oh, tell my mother and sister that from now on I shall not only be inside them, but also for them, for them, for them."

Yesterday his niece, Holly, asked me, "In Heaven do they eat food?" I told her, "Certainly they do." Now I am sure all of you know that here on earth we eat. Also in Heaven, in the vital world, we eat. The food is different from ours. It is like tiny particles of sugar, which have a very grey colour. About seventeen years ago, one of my sisters, who was very fond of me, died. The first time I entered into that vital world she gave me that food. I said, "I cannot eat it. It is all bone; I don't want to eat bone." She laughed and laughed, and made me eat. Just last night I was given this food by Buddy, and beside him were my mother and my friend and a few friends of his. We were all sitting, dining. So those who believe in the inner life, the spiritual life, will immediately believe that this inner world is also a world of reality. There we talk, we eat, we do everything.

Later the children asked, "How can we talk to him?" I answered, "Here on earth, no matter how far away we are from someone, we can talk to him on the telephone. Similarly, there is another kind of telephone to speak to people in Heaven." This other telephone is the capacity of the soul's oneness. All of us—not only in the land of dreams or the world of spirit, but also in this world of reality—can enter into our departed ones while meditating. But unfortunately we do not do this. We live in the physical and do not go beyond the boundaries of the physical. That is why we do not feel our dearest ones after they depart. But if we go deep into our meditation, we will be able to see them concretely, right in front of our eyes.

Right now Buddy's soul is in the world of the moon, considered to be one of the highest realms in the spiritual world. There are many, many worlds, but this world of the moon is full of purest joy, delight and tranquility. Soon Buddy will be with us again. In a few years we will see him in a different body, and I will be able to tell you that Buddy's soul has reincarnated in a different form. I told him that his mother, sister, brother, father and all of his dear ones want to see him. He said, "See me? They will get me." So they will get him in a different form, in a different body.

CHAPTER 4

Death and Life:
Two Inseparable Brothers

The following two sets of aphorisms, written by Sri Chinmoy in India in 1962, are taken from his book Eternity's Breath.

DEATH

Death is natural. Nothing natural can be detrimental. Death is rest. Rest is strength in disguise for a further adventure.

At the present stage of human evolution, to conquer death may be an impossibility. But to overcome the fear of death is not only a practicability, but an inevitability.

Death is normally the sign that the soul, under the particular circumstances, has exhausted the possibilities of its progress in a particular body.

When the strength of possibility loses to the strength of impossibility, it is called death.

A useless life is a cordial invitation to death.

Death is the hyphen between man's growing fear and his shrinking life-energies.

He who prefers death to life has only to climb up the tree. But he who prefers life to death has not only to climb up, but also to climb down again to do God's work.

When death approaches a man, his psychic being says to death, "Death, just wait, let me see what I wish to work out in the next birth." Death says, "Sorry, you are asking a favour from the wrong person. One second's delay on my part may add something valuable to your experience of this life."

Death says that it is immortal. Man's achievements say, "Death, you are right. But the truth of the matter is that we shine perpetually upon your very breast. Not only that, we shine forever in you, through you and beyond you."

LIFE

Life is love. Love is life. Life fulfils God through love. Love fulfils God in life.

Life has an inner door. Aspiration opens it. Desire closes it. Aspiration opens the door from within. Desire closes it from without.

Life has an inner lamp. This inner lamp is called aspiration. And when we keep our aspiration burning, it will, without fail, transmit to God's entire creation its effulgent glow.

Life has an inner voice. This voice is the Light of the Supreme. Life is protection, life is perfection, life is fulfilment when we open to this Light of the Supreme.

God is in life. But life must awaken to the Light of His Presence, His Transcendental Feet.

Each day is the renewal of life. Each day is the rebirth of our inner assurance that each individual is the chosen instrument of the Supreme to reveal and fulfil the infinite Divine here on earth.

The outgoing life finds nothing but trouble, torture, misery and frustration. The inflowing life discovers the sea of peace and bliss.

To illumine our life we need pure thoughts. Each pure thought is more precious than all the diamonds of the world, for God's Breath abides only in man's pure thoughts.

How to start life's inner journey? With the simple idea, the spontaneous thought that God-realisation is your birthright. Where to start? Here, from within. When to start? Now, before the birth of another second.

Life is always at work. It is ever active, dynamic. It tries to help the soul to complete its yet unaccomplished task, the divine Mission. The soul needs life's help to unfold itself fully. Life needs the soul's help to fulfil itself both physically and spiritually.

Brooding and despondency are the worst foes to kill life in all its divine inspiration. No more brooding, no more despondency. Your life shall become the beauty of a rose, the song of the dawn, the dance of the twilight.

Birth and death play. They play together. Their game is the game of harmony. And it is always played on the infinite breast of life.

CHAPTER 5

Life after Death:
The Higher and Lower Worlds

Is there life after death?

Life after death is inevitable. If there were only one life on earth, then it would be impossible for us to accomplish the things that we have to accomplish. God, being all Satisfaction, will not allow us to remain unsatisfied. He will always want us to be fully satisfied. In one incarnation we cannot fulfil our aspiration; we cannot reach the Highest. So here we have life and then we pass through a tunnel which we call death. There we take a little rest and then we come back again. If there were no reincarnation, then no soul would be able to manifest the ultimate Truth. In one incarnation it is impossible.

You said that in a way our body is like a shell for our soul and that in due time our body will die and rot. What happens to the soul? What does it do? How far does it go?

The soul never dies. The soul is the immortal thing within us. It is the body that dies. At death the soul gradually goes back to its own region. As soon as the body dies, the physical enters into the physical world, the vital enters into the vital world, the mind enters into the mental world and the heart enters into the psychic world.

The soul goes back to the soul's region for a short rest. There are seven higher worlds, like seven rungs of the spiritual ladder, and seven lower worlds. The moment the soul leaves the body it climbs up one rung and then goes up, up, up and covers the seven rungs of consciousness of the seven higher worlds. Then finally it enters into the sea of immense peace. There it takes rest. The length of the rest depends on the individual soul. Some souls come back into the world after six years or ten years or twelve years. The more advanced a soul is, the longer it takes to return. In the case of an ordinary soul which has not been able to manifest much or offer much to the earth, it usually comes back in about six years' time from the soul's region. But if the soul is very advanced, as in the case of great spiritual Masters, it comes only once in three hundred, four hundred years. And again, if it is the Will of the Supreme, then even a very advanced spiritual person is bound to come again after fifteen years or twenty years.

Before it comes back into the world of manifestation, it goes to the Lord Supreme for an interview. They have a heart-to-heart talk. The soul tells how much it has achieved in its previous incarnation and the Supreme tells it how much it has to achieve in its next incarnation. When the Supreme tells the soul what to do, He gives the necessary power and light to the soul.

Each time the soul comes down, like a divine soldier it enters into the battlefield of life and fights against doubt, obscurity, ignorance, imperfection, limitations, worries and so forth. It tries to reveal its own inner divinity and establish the divine Truth on earth according to its capacity. And then, at the end of its journey's close in a particular incarnation it goes back to its own region. When the time comes to return, it tells the Supreme what it is intending to do, and the Supreme either sanctions or disapproves of its plan. Sometimes if the soul is not absolutely clear in its judgement, the Supreme throws abundant light on the soul.

What happens to the vital at the hour of death?

There are two vitals. One is the physical vital, the vital that is in the physical. The other is the vital proper, the vital which does not belong to the physical. It is not identified with the physical; it is totally separate. When the soul leaves the body, the human being decomposes into its five elements. The vital proper enters into the vital sheath. The mind stays for a short while with the vital, for a few days or a few months, and then it goes back to the mind's level, the mental sheath. The soul stays in the vital sheath for two months, six months, sometimes even a few years; it depends on the individual soul. Then it passes to the mental world and then to the psychic world.

When the vital is in the vital sheath, it may suffer considerably. If the vital is unlit and impure, then it is tortured there most mercilessly. When our third eye is open, we see that no human punishment is as severe or as cruel as the vital punishment. Again, if the vital has aspired in its own way to be one with the soul, if the vital listened to the soul when the seeker was on earth, then the vital does not suffer in the vital zone. If the individual is spiritually advanced, he suffers practically nothing, because he knows the ins and outs of that realm. If a spiritual Master intervenes he can very rapidly take a soul to the other inner worlds. The fastest that a spiritual Master can do this is nineteen days.

In the vital itself there are higher worlds and there are lower worlds. On earth we have countries, and there they are called worlds. Here we say that some countries are bad and other countries are nice. All the inner worlds other than the vital are good worlds, although some are higher than others. But in the vital, some worlds are not so nice. The higher the soul goes, from the lower vital to the higher vital to the psychic worlds, the better for it. In the higher inner worlds souls have better treatment and better nourishment. Everything is better.

Do the circumstances under which a person dies determine where he goes after he leaves the body?

That depends mainly on the consciousness of the individual, and this consciousness is the gradually accumulated achievement of his entire life. My good disciples will go to a very high plane immediately if they can think of me at the time of death. If a mother is killed while protecting her child, her soul will go to a high world. When a soldier dies defending his country if his country is attacked, he will go to a high world.

In India there was a time when the wives threw themselves into the funeral pyre of their husbands. People may say that this is suicide, and granted it is. But in these cases the wives did not go to the lower inconscient worlds where people who commit suicide usually go. These wives had tremendous love and devotion for, and oneness with, their husbands, and God blessed their divine qualities and granted them the Grace to go to the worlds where they would otherwise have gone according to the development of their souls.

Again, there were other wives who were forced to do this by law. They did it out of fear, out of necessity, but not out of a feeling of love or oneness. For them, too, the treatment was not the same in the inner world as for those who willfully committed suicide. They, too, went to their respective places according to their soul's standard. But those who gave their lives out of joy and oneness naturally created a strong connection with their husbands which will be maintained in future lives.

When we go to the other world after leaving the body, are there any forms or is it all formless?

When somebody dies, if the soul wants to come and see the relatives still on earth, the soul usually takes the form that it had on earth so that the relatives can recognise it. But great spiritual Masters can recognise the soul no matter what form it takes. Even if the soul takes the form of a column of light, the Master can use his third eye and immediately recognise the soul.

What happens to the souls that have retired from work on earth? Will they eventually fill up the other worlds?

There is lots of room in the other worlds. There we deal with Infinity.

What happens to the soul of an animal after it leaves the body?

It has its own world. Each soul has its own capacity. The soul of a saint will not go to the same place as the soul of a thief. The saint will go to a much higher world. It all depends on the consciousness that the soul has revealed here on earth. So, animals will go to a world that will suit them. They will not go to a world where the souls are very highly developed.

Do our souls ever leave our bodies for just a second while we are alive?

For a few seconds during the day the soul may leave, but the consciousness of the soul remains in the body at that time. This is your room and your whole vibration is here. As soon as somebody comes here, he will immediately feel your vibration. But if you go away and do not come back, then there will be nothing here. If the soul stays away, then its own body becomes foreign; its own room is foreign. But when it is a matter of dying, the body, like a cage, is broken. So what is the use of staying in a broken cage?

I have heard that seeing the relatives' and friends' tears gives great joy to the soul when parting from this life. Is this true?

In general there are three types of human souls: first there are what we call most ordinary, unenlightened; then good but ordinary souls; then great, extraordinary souls. When an ordinary man dies, he looks all around to see whether his dear and near ones are crying for him. If he sees that nobody is crying, then he gets terribly disheartened and says to himself: "All my life I have helped them in various ways. Now look at this ingratitude!" These ordinary souls are so attached to their dear ones and so attached to earth that they become disheartened if at this last moment their dear ones do not acknowledge their previous love and sacrifice. There are even some unenlightened souls that take a malicious attitude if their relatives do not mourn for them and come back in disembodied form to frighten their dear ones after they have left the body. If there are children in the family, the deceased may assume the ugliest form and come in front of the children to frighten them.

The second type of person has been nice, sweet and extremely helpful to the members of his family, and when he is about to die he feels that there should be a bond of affection and attachment which lasts forever. This kind of person does not want to leave the earth-scene. He feels that it is attachment alone that can maintain the connection between this world and the other world, so he tries to draw the utmost affection and sympathy and concern from his dear and near ones. If he sees that his dear and near ones are not showing any sympathy or sorrow for his loss, or are not crying bitterly, then he gets a tremendous pang in his inner existence. He feels: "Here I want to establish something permanently, and I am not getting any help or coopera-tion from the members of my family." But it is not the so-called human love, it is not human attachment, that can create an eternal divine bond between the departed soul and the souls that are in the land of the living. The love that binds human beings can never last; it is like a rope of sand. It is only the divine love that can tran-scend all barriers.

Then we come to great souls, that is to say, spiritual Masters. When a Master leaves the body and sees that his disciples are crying bitterly over their loss, the Master feels sorry because the disciples do not recog-nise him fully as a spiritual Master. A spiritual person, one who has realised God, lives on all planes; his con-sciousness pervades all the worlds. So if his disciples cry bitterly for him, feeling that they will see him no more, then they are putting their Master in the same category as an ordinary person. It is like an insult. The Master knows that he will appear before the disciples who are sincerely praying to him or who are meditating and aspiring sincerely. He knows that he will be all the time guiding, shaping and moulding them. He knows that he will be able to enter into them, and they will be able to enter into him. So naturally he feels sad if his disciples take the attitude: "Now the Master is gone and we will never hear him again. Our prayers to him will be in vain, so it is useless to pray. Let us go to some other Master or let us try to find another means to make spiritual progress." So spiritual Masters feel sorry when their dearest ones cry or shed bitter tears for them, whereas ordinary people get joy from this.

Yes, for a while the disciples can feel sad that they have lost their Master, that they will not see him in the physical frame. But that sadness must not last because the soul's joy, the soul's intense love and all-pervading concern, have to enter into the disciples who have sincerely accepted the Master as the sole pilot of their lives.

Do spiritual Masters ever appear in the subtle body after their death?

In India, many spiritual Masters have proved to their dear ones that death is not the end by appearing most vividly in the subtle body. Just one example I will give you. There was a great spiritual Master named Sri Ramakrishna. When he left the body, his wife became a widow. It is customary in India that when the husband dies, the wife stops wearing her bangles and jewels. But when Sri Ramakrishna's wife was removing her jewelry, her husband appeared before her so vividly and said to her, "What are you doing? You should not take off these bangles and jewels. On the contrary, from now on you should wear golden bracelets and golden jewelry. I am now immortal. Therefore, you should wear something more beautiful, more meaningful and more fruitful." There are many incidents like that, only they are not recorded.

Does the soul ever linger on earth after death in order to help its near and dear ones?

Some souls don't waste much time. They just go away. They only wait for a few days to see if their relatives and friends care for them. After three or four days they have experienced enough.

Again, some wise souls stay in spite of being very bright and powerful. They want to see if they can help their friends and relatives before they enter into the mental world. If they can be of some service to their dear ones, they do it. They help them in many ways by inspiring them. Sometimes they come to a friend or relative in a dream with some light, and they give some inspiration. Or they come to them and say, "There is nothing lasting on earth. As I have left the body, so also you will have to leave. My time is expired. Now I can't do anything more for God on earth. So the best thing is to achieve something for God on earth. Don't waste time. Do as much as you can." Before it leaves the body, each soul feels sorry that it has wasted time. We all waste time. The soul can also give people answers either through luck or through inner communication. So there are many ways the soul can help its near and dear ones.

Why do people keep the body for a few hours or even for a few days after the soul has departed?

You can say it is because the relatives want to see the remains. They feel sorry because this body, this person, helped them or loved them during life. The father does not see the mother's soul during her lifetime, but he sees her body, so he is attached to the physical. That is why, when she dies, he wants to keep the physical as long as he can. When the soul has left, the body is useless. It is just like the old, dirty dress you put in the wastebasket. If it is an ordinary soul, after it leaves the body, it hovers in the house or in the yard or somewhere nearby. God gives the soul a chance to see whether the family really cared for it, and the soul gives the family a chance to show whether they actually cared about its death. Then after a few hours, usually about eleven hours although it may be longer, the soul departs and does not come back again.

Even if a seeker hasn't realised God while on earth, will his soul see God or realise God after it leaves the body?

Every soul is bound to see God, because the soul must come directly from God. When the soul leaves the body, it goes to the vital world, the mental world, the psychic world and finally to the soul's own world. Here it rests for a while. Then, before it comes down for its next incarnation, the soul will have an interview with God. The soul has to stand in front of the Supreme and say how much it has achieved in its past incarnation. It will see the possibilities of its coming incarnation and make promises to the Supreme. The aims and ideals that the soul expresses for its role in the world of revelation and manifestation have to be approved by the Supreme. Sometimes the Supreme Himself says: "I expect this from you. Try to accomplish it for My sake there on earth."

The soul that sees God and has a conversation with Him is like a stranger to us, for most of us have not seen the soul on earth. Unless we have free access to the soul, unless we hear the voice of the soul and try to listen to its inner dictates, it is simply impossible for us to realise God. After it leaves the body, every soul will see God in the sense that I see you because I am standing in front of you. But the thing is that when one realises God in the physical, here on earth, it is a totally different matter. Here the whole consciousness—the physical consciousness, the individual consciousness—merges into the infinite Light and Bliss. When we read spiritual books or listen to others, we may feel that God is ours. But our conscious oneness is something else. When we consciously feel God as our very own, then at every moment in our inner life, our inner existence, we feel boundless peace. Outwardly we may be excited or talking, but in our inner life we are a sea of peace, light and delight. When this sea of peace, light and delight comes into our physical being, our physical consciousness, then our inner divinity can be manifested on earth. In Heaven we cannot manifest anything, and also, we cannot realise anything. If the soul does not realise God while it is here on earth in the shackles of the finite, it will not realise God when it is in its own world. Realisation can only be achieved through the physical.

Guru, will we see you when we leave the body?

If you are my true disciple, you are bound to see me when you leave the body. That much I assure you. If you are my real disciple, you will not be able to die without my knowledge and consent. At that time I will stand right in front of you and take you in my chariot. I will carry you in a golden or silver or bronze chariot. You will see. This is the promise that great spiritual Masters give: they will come and take the souls of their disciples.

Will we see you after you leave the body?

You may see me in a dream for a minute or two. Spiritual Masters, when they leave the body, often open the third eye of their disciples for a few minutes.

Will everyone see you in the inner world after death?

The soul's region is a big place, a vast place. The earth is also a vast place. If you had not come to my Centre, I would not have seen you. In the inner world I move from one place to another. Now if my real headquarters is on the plane that a person is on, then certainly that person will see me. We will have a group of people there who truly love me and are sincerely devoted to me. We will dwell together in the same plane. But those who do not care for me, those who know nothing about me and have no connection with me will not see me, unless it is the express Will of the Supreme. Those people will see others at their own level of development. They will dwell with the ones whom they loved.

Many people who have close calls with death often report a similar experience—coming face to face

with a luminous being or a light which gives them a message. What are these beings?

Sometimes they are not beings at all, but the souls of deceased relatives. Sometimes they are old and friendly acquaintances from previous incarnations. Sometimes they are fate-making angels or deities. Sometimes they are fruitful imaginations of the seeker's soulful aspiration.

A friend of mine, a lady who was very spiritual, passed away recently. Will her friends come to meet her in a beautiful Heaven?

If her friends were also spiritual and highly developed, naturally they will come to receive her if they themselves are still in Heaven. But if her friends left the body long before she did, who knows where they are now? They may be in the region of Heaven, or they may be still loitering in the vital plane, or they may have taken human incarnation already. But if they have passed through the vital world, the mental world and a few other worlds, and are now enjoying the blissful rest of Heaven, and if the souls still maintain their same sweet feeling for your friend, then naturally they will come to receive her and help her enjoy a life of bliss in Heaven.

My own mother happened to be a very, very spiritual woman. When my mother was leaving the body, a very close relative of mine saw in a dream that my mother's friends were coming in a golden chariot to receive her. When my father died, one of my uncles, who was away in the city, saw another uncle of mine and a few other people coming to take my father in a golden boat. There were many to receive my father and mother because both they and many of their friends and relatives were very spiritual.

In the case of almost all religious and spiritual people, the relatives do come. It is easier for spiritual people to come, because they have almost a free access to this world. When ordinary people who are not spiritual and aspiring leave the body, they do not go immediately to God. They stay in the vital world and suffer a great deal. When one disciple's father died, he went to the vital world where he was not treated well. He was having quite a few problems there until one of the vital beings asked him if he had known any religious or spiritual people in his life. He said, "Yes, I know my daughter's friend"—who happened to be me. When my name was said, immediately the vital beings knew whom he was connected with, so he was released immediately. He was then able to leave the vital world, the world of torture, and go to a very good higher world.

When another disciple's father died, he went to a very high place, but he was not satisfied there. Her father had seen me only once, in Canada, but when he had, his whole body had been thrilled from head to foot with ineffable joy. So when he left the body and was not satisfied with the plane he was in, his soul came to me and said, "I want to go to a higher world." So I called on one of my friends, Jyotish, to take him to the plane where he was living. Now he is extremely happy there, in this very high world. He sometimes comes to me and expresses his deepest joy.

When he takes his next incarnation I will know about it. Most probably he will take incarnation in an Italian family, but it depends absolutely on the Will of the Supreme. And of course there will be a little bit of my interference if he wants to go somewhere which I do not approve of. Sometimes souls make mistakes when they decide upon their next incarnation. If the souls are very close to my heart, I do not allow them to do this. Right now as I am talking to you, believe me, I am getting an inner vibration from her father that he wants to come into the family of one of our disciples. For the first time now, he sees an inner link. Before this he wanted to come into an Italian family, but now, as I am speaking, in the inner world he is sending me the message that he wants to come into one of our disciples' families. Nothing will give us greater joy than to have him with us. And let us see what the other father does after taking a little rest.

Will the soul be able to have some kinds of experiences in the worlds it goes to after it leaves the body?

As soon as the soul leaves this physical body, the physical body will be dissolved in matter. The body enters into the physical sheath, the vital enters into the vital sheath and the mind enters into the mental plane proper. The soul will go through the subtle physical, the vital, the mental, the psychic and then finally to the soul's own region. As it passes through each of these planes, the soul takes up with it the essence of all the experiences it had on earth.

The soul gets various kinds of subtle experiences in these other sheaths, but these experiences are not going to manifest in these worlds. If the soul gets some experience here on earth, the experience is bound to be manifested either today or tomorrow. In the soul's world there is no manifestation. Progress is there, but not in the sense of evolution.

We enter into the soul's world to take rest. But if our soul associates with a higher soul, a more illumined soul, then naturally we will be inspired. If, in the soul's world, we are near a spiritual Master or some other very great, significant, spiritual person, then naturally we will be influenced. The soul can aspire in any world. In the higher worlds it will have only aspiration, and this aspiration will eventually take the form of experience. Aspiration itself is an experience. But on earth, when the soul observes suffering or joy or the activities of the world, the experiences that the soul gets here are constantly leading it towards the fuller manifestation of divinity.

When the soul leaves the body after death, you said it enters into the vital sphere. What is the vital sphere?

The vital sphere or region is simply a world, and that world is also within us. As we have the physical world, so also we have the vital world, the mental world, the psychic world, the soul's world and other worlds. When we go within, immediately after the physical is the vital world. This vital is operating every day in us. Sometimes our physical consciousness will enter into the vital; other times the vital world enters into the physical. Very often we enter into the vital world in our dreams. When the soul passes from one plane of consciousness to another in our dreams, the first plane it enters into when it leaves the physical is the vital. And when the soul leaves the body and the person dies, the first step on the soul's journey towards its own resting place, its destination, is the vital world. Some souls suffer there, while others do not. It is like visiting a strange, new country. Some are fortunate enough to mix freely with the people of the new country and understand its culture in almost no time, while others are not so fortunate.

The vital that we have embodied here in this physical is something solid. With our physical eyes we cannot see the vital, but in our feelings, in our inner perception, we can feel it. Again, with our human eyes we can actually see the vital movement and activity here on earth. This vital can take and has taken the real form of a subtle body. When the soul leaves the body and the body stops functioning, this form becomes formless; the vital form that we had during our lifetime enters into the vital sheath. The vital which had form enters into the formless vital. There it takes rest or disintegrates, while the soul travels back to its own region.

What is it like in the vital world?

In the vital world immediately after the physical world, there is tremendous chaos and restlessness, insecurity, obscurity, dissatisfaction and a sense of incompleteness. Nevertheless, a tremendous power is operating in and through all these forces. This world is a portion of the passage through which the souls come into the physical world before birth and return to the higher worlds after death. This vital world is very chaotic. If you go there, you will see many broken and deformed things, as though a cyclone has hit the area. In this particular vital world the migrating beings are not usually happy. They become happy only when they have passed through it and entered into a higher vital world where a conscious aim and an upward urge are palpable.

Is hell really a place in the vital worlds, or is it just a state of consciousness?

On the physical-mental level, hell is a place. It is for the soul's experience. If you lead a bad life you have to go there. There it is real torture, unimaginable torture. Especially for those who commit suicide, the torture is infinitely worse than being fried alive in oil. The suffering that suicides go through in the subtle physical and subtle vital is unthinkable, unbearable. They will not get another incarnation for a long time. Then after suffering in the vital world for many years, when they finally do get an incarnation, they will be defective: blind, paralysed, mongoloid and all kinds of things. And this is not just for one incarnation, either. If they are not forgiven by a spiritual Master or by God's Grace, this will go on for quite a few incarnations. Not only that, but right from the beginning they create a disturbance for the entire family that they are born into. For instance, if a suicide takes incarnation and is insane, he will cause serious problems for his whole family. Also, these souls often increase their own bad karma because they go on in the same way and they do not change. But if there is Grace from God, or if a spiritual Master intervenes, the soul is helped.

So when we live in the gross physical consciousness or in the body-consciousness, hell is really a place. But on the highest spiritual level, we have to know that hell, as well as Heaven, is a plane of consciousness. Both Heaven and hell begin in the mind. The moment we think something good, the moment we pray and meditate and try to offer the inner light that we have gained from our meditation and prayers, we begin to live in Heaven. The moment we think evil of someone, criticise someone and cherish wrong thoughts about someone, then we enter into hell. Heaven we create; hell we create. With our divine thoughts we create Heaven. With our wrong, silly, undivine thoughts, we create hell within us. Heaven and hell are both states of consciousness deep inside us. When we go deep within, we see that the entire universe is inside us. Inside this physical body is the subtle body, and inside the subtle body, in the heart, we find the existence of the soul. Then, from there, if we go deep within, we see the entire universe.

If someone is violently killed, does his soul undergo the same suffering as that of someone who has committed suicide?

No, it is not the same. If someone becomes a victim in a war or if someone is violently killed in a car accident, then it is some wrong forces that have killed the person. On the other hand, if somebody destroys his body, he becomes the aggressor. So the victim and the aggressor cannot be in the same category.

What if a political prisoner commits suicide to end the unbearable suffering? Would that person have the same punishment as someone who simply takes his own life in a mood of escapism?

It depends on merits and demerits. During the war, how inhumanly and brutally the people in concentration camps were tortured and killed. What if they themselves wanted to destroy their lives because they didn't want to be killed or mercilessly beaten without any reason? Here we have to know that there is something called God's dispensation. Let us say that these people are innocent

73

and they are being killed. Or they fought for their lives and lost and now they are being killed. In order not to be killed by the enemy, they may want to destroy themselves.

In India and elsewhere it has happened many times that two warriors are fighting, and one knows definitely that the other one has won and it is a matter of a minute or a second before he will be destroyed. Immediately he will put an end to his life. His suffering will not be the same as if he had just committed suicide.

Will the soul suffer if a person commits hara-kiri, a form of suicide which is regarded as honourable in Japan?

It entirely depends on the individual case. Ordinarily, people commit suicide because they cannot face reality; they have emotional problems or their desires are not fulfilled. But each case is different and only God can decide. In the case of spiritual Masters, they can leave the body at will. But they do not harm the physical. The soul leaves occultly and spiritually. But first they take permission from the Supreme.

If someone makes an almost impossible attempt to save someone else's life and he dies in the attempt, is this like suicide?

You have to know the motive. The mother sees that the child is drowning. She may not be able to know that it is God's intention that she stay on earth and look after her other children. Only she sees that her son is drowning, so she tries to save him. Then, if she dies, this is not suicide.

Can someone whose soul was in hell go to Heaven?

The usual process is that first he has to go to earth and do good things. But hell is only a portion of the vital world, so from there it is possible to go directly to Heaven. If they get direct help from the Supreme or from a spiritual Master, some souls can go from hell to Heaven. Otherwise, they have to come back to earth and acquire spiritual merits.

CHAPTER 6

Reincarnation:
The Great Pilgrimage

What is the purpose of reincarnation?

In one lifetime on earth we cannot do everything. If we remain in the world of desire, we will never be able to fulfil ourselves. As a child we have millions of desires, and even when we reach the age of seventy we see that a particular desire has not been fulfilled and we feel miserable. The more desires we fulfil, the more desires we get. We want one house, then two houses; one car, then two cars, and so forth. There is no limit to it. When our desires are fulfilled, we find that we are still dissatisfied. Then we become the victims of other desires or larger desires.

Now our dearest is God. Do you think that God will allow us to remain unfulfilled? No! God's very purpose is to fulfil each individual, and Himself through us. He will have us come back again and again to fulfil our desires. If someone is eager to become a millionaire in this incarnation, and at the end of his journey he sees that he has not become a millionaire, then if his desire is really intense, he will have to keep coming back until he really becomes a millionaire. But by becoming a millionaire, he will see that he still remains a beggar in one sense, for he will have no peace of mind. If he enters into the world of aspiration, he may have no money, but he will have peace of mind, and this is the real wealth.

If we live in the world of desire, we see that there is an endless procession of desires. But if we live in the world of aspiration, we see the whole, we enter into the whole and eventually we become the whole. We know that if we can realise God, inside God we will find everything, for everything exists inside God. So eventually we leave the world of desire and enter into the world of aspiration. There we diminish our desires and think more of peace, bliss and divine love. In order to get a little peace, a drop of nectar, it may take years and years. But a spiritual person is ready to wait indefinitely for God's Hour to fulfil his aspiration. And his aspiration to achieve this peace, light and bliss will not go in vain.

Now if our aim is to enter into the Highest, the Infinite, the Eternal, the Immortal, then naturally one short span of life is not enough. But again, God will not allow us to remain unfulfilled. In our next incarnation we will continue our journey. We are eternal travellers. We have to continue, continue until we reach our Goal. Perfection is the aim of each individual. We are trying to perfect ourselves in an imperfect world. And this perfect perfection we can never have in one life.

It is through aspiration and evolution that the soul develops the full possibility of realising the Highest and fulfilling the Divine. The physical, the human in us, has to aspire to become one with the Divine in us—the soul. Right now the body does not listen to the dictates of the soul; that is to say, the physical mind revolts.

The workings of the physical mind cover up the soul's divine purpose, and the soul cannot come to the fore. At the present stage of evolution, most people are unconscious and do not know what the soul wants or needs. They have desires, anxiety over success, intensity and excitement. All these stem from the vital or ego, whereas anything done with the soul's consciousness is always all joy. At times we may hear the dictates of the soul, or the message of our conscience, but still we do not do or say the right thing. No, the physical mind is weak; we are weak. If we start aspiring, however, with the mind, and then go beyond the mind to the soul, we can easily hear and also obey the dictates of the soul.

A day will come when the soul is in a position to exercise its divine qualities and make the body, mind and heart feel that they need their self-discovery. The physical and the vital will consciously want to listen to the soul and be instructed and guided by the soul. Then, here in the physical, we will have an immortalised nature, an immortal life, for our soul will have become totally and inseparably one with the Divine on earth. At that time we will offer our inner wealth to the world at large and manifest our soul's potentialities. It very often happens that realisation can take place in one incarnation, but for manifestation the soul has to come down again and again to earth. Unless and until we reveal and manifest the highest Divinity within us, our game is not over. We have not finished our role in the Cosmic Drama, so we have to come back into the world again and again. But in the march of evolution, in one of its incarnations, the soul will fully realise and fully manifest the Divine in the physical and through the physical.

You said that we are all evolving and progressing. But where did this whole process start? Was there a beginning?

We came into existence from God's Delight. When we entered the creation, we evolved through the lower stages: mineral life, plant life, animal life. Although we have now entered into the human life, we are still half animal. There are some who want to kill or hurt others, and exhibit all kinds of animal and destructive tendencies.

But in the case of a spiritual aspirant, it is different. He tries to dispose of his lower nature and aspires to be aware of and live in his divine nature, where he experiences peace, joy and love.

In the beginning we came from Delight; we are now growing in Delight; and we shall consciously return to Delight.

Why did we go from light to darkness when we took birth?

Actually we did not go from light to darkness when we entered into the world. It is a very complicated matter. Each birth is part of the process of evolution. Each person has a soul. The soul enters into matter and from matter it aspires. Mother-Earth has the inner urge, the aspiration to be one with the Highest, the cosmic Self, and eventually all human beings on earth will become one with the highest Spirit. This is an evolutionary process leading towards perfect perfection. Some will say that God is everywhere; God is inside us and likewise God is inside a thief. When He is not in creation but beyond creation, He is all Light and He enjoys the Light of the Beyond. But when He enters into manifestation, He wants to enjoy Himself in a million ways. The Cosmic Self wants to fulfil its Cosmic Play in each individual and in each creature here on earth. For that, evolution is proceeding.

Our soul is all light. But on earth the atmosphere is not aspiring. When somebody takes birth, the first thing he sees is ignorance and illusion all around. In the highest plane we are all perfect, but now in the material plane, we are experiencing the play of ignorance. During our meditation we raise our level of consciousness a little, and find ourselves hundreds of miles above the bed of thorns. Yet, if we remain only where our meditation takes us, above the thorns, and if we cry for perfection, our cry is only partially fulfilled. We are not eating the full fruit. God is inside everything. He must be realised in the material plane also.

In the deepest philosophy, what we call night is not absolutely night. There is some light there also. A person who is realised naturally has more inner light than a person who is not realised. The world will say that the unrealised person is all ignorance because he has not realised God. We are always comparing someone with someone else. What is really happening is that we are growing from little light to more light, to abundant light, each according to his own understanding and capacity. What we call night is also light in an infinitesimal form. It is because we are marching forward that we see the difference between effulgent light and darkest night. Strictly speaking, in everything there is light. Our human understanding makes us see both light and darkness. But from the highest point of view we should always feel that we are marching from light to more light, to abundant light.

How does the Supreme incarnate on earth? Does He use evolution or something else?

All the possibilities have taken place. Sometimes He has literally taken a human body and gone through birth. Other times He has projected a portion of the body. Sometimes He is eighty percent upstairs in the higher worlds and twenty percent downstairs on the earth plane, and other times He wants to be one hundred percent conscious both upstairs and downstairs. It is as if someone is living on the first floor, but has access to the whole building. Sometimes He incarnates with His whole Consciousness and sometimes with a portion of His Consciousness.

When God began His creation, higher souls occasionally took incarnation in one of four or five types of forms. Sometimes cosmic gods took a human form directly. They did not go through the animal process. Then afterwards, the gods would not take human incarnation again because they were satisfied. The cosmic gods did not care for realisation, which has to be achieved through evolution on earth; they cared only for limited power. Of course, this limited power is infinitely more powerful than the power any human being can have.

So there was no one process of evolution for the higher souls. Some began from the mineral and some from the animal kingdom. Some took human incarnations immediately. If all spiritual Masters had started with the animal form, then God alone knows how spiritual evolution would have taken place.

Is there a special evolution for advanced souls?

A holy man in his next incarnation can become a Yogi, and then he can become a real spiritual Master. In each life he will only increase his capacity. Each time he becomes stronger, so he will dare to challenge and transform ignorance more. First, as a holy man, he is afraid and does not want to challenge ignorance. He feels that he will lose his purity and divinity. Then, when he becomes a spiritual Master, he is not at all afraid; he knows he can dare to accept it because he has the capacity to transform it. Even without touching it, he can throw ignorance into the Universal Consciousness and he can transform the nature of humanity. He starts as a holy man. There he is strengthened and his power has increased infinitely. Each time it increases, he becomes a greater manifestation, a greater perfection, a greater fulfilment of the Supreme.

Must a person evolve in every incarnation?

Each incarnation is meant for progress. Either you can take one step or ten steps or ten million steps. Progress depends on how much aspiration one has. Each incarnation indicates that the soul is entering into the world arena to manifest something. The soul enters into the physical. It has made a fervent promise to God, but because of earthly pleasures and human ignorance, the soul finds it very difficult to make progress. In each life the soul comes to the physical with one sincere will: to go forward. So each incarnation is meant for that. The only thing is that some can cover only one step with greatest difficulty while others can take countless steps. Each incarnation is meant for gradual progress.

Your philosophy states that the soul is always making progress, but how do you reconcile that with the fact that when someone commits suicide his soul falls?

When one commits suicide the soul of that person actually does not fall. But it remains at a particular place and is covered by infinitely more veils of ignorance. It is absolutely covered by ignorance—layer upon layer of ignorance. It is the consciousness of the individual that falls. It goes backwards right to the starting point, almost to the mineral consciousness where there is no evolution. The soul is eclipsed by teeming ignorance, that is to say, by infinite layers of ignorance. Before, the soul had perhaps ten layers, but now it has countless layers of ignorance. The soul has to begin again removing them one by one. Of course, it becomes infinitely more difficult for the soul to carry the individual to perfect perfection, liberation or salvation.

But if the Supreme wants to operate in a particular human being who has committed suicide, on very, very rare occasions, the Supreme asks the spiritual Masters, who have the capacity, to take care of that soul and not to allow it to be enveloped by teeming ignorance. In these cases, whatever the soul already has is enough to bring the Grace and Compassion of the Supreme, and He will not allow a veil to cover the soul more than usual. But this is done only on very rare occasions.

Otherwise, if a person commits suicide, evolution stops for that individual indefinitely—for one hundred, two hundred, five hundred, six hundred years or even more. He cannot go forward, and the heaviest possible load is placed on his shoulders. The process of his evolution stops. Because he has violated the laws of the

Cosmic Game, he has to undergo the cosmic punishment. This punishment can never be imagined by any human being on earth. The worst possible earthly torture is simply nothing in comparison to the cosmic punishment the individual gets when he commits suicide. You cannot say to the cosmic forces, "I have done something wrong and it is none of your business. I shall reach my goal when I feel like reaching it." You have jumped out of the Cosmic Game intentionally, without God's permission and against His intention. He has not allowed you to leave the game, but you have actively and openly defied Him and tried to ruin the game. For this wrong action the punishment is most severe. This punishment is so intense that with our human heart we cannot feel it, with our human mind we cannot imagine it.

Do you have the divine power to reduce the number of our future incarnations?

Most of the sincere, dedicated disciples have already made such progress in the spiritual life that they have eliminated the need for quite a few incarnations. First class disciples have already made such progress that although it will take them many more incarnations to realise God, they will be realised much sooner than they would have otherwise been.

It depends on how fast you run. If you are a slow runner it will take you forty or fifty seconds to run one hundred metres. But a first-class runner will do it in eleven seconds because he has the capacity to run faster. If someone has the eagerness to learn from a coach or an instructor, naturally he will run the fastest. But if somebody does not practise or take instruction from the coach, then how will he run as fast as someone who does? So speed is of utmost importance. In the case of running a race, it is a matter of ten or twenty or thirty seconds. But in the case of the spiritual life, it is a matter of ten or twenty or forty or sixty incarnations. If you run the fastest when a spiritual Master enters into your life, at that time you have a golden opportunity. All spiritual Masters have said that when spiritual figures descend, it is like an oceanliner that can carry many people very fast. The individual seeker is like a little tiny boat that may capsize at any moment.

Is it possible that this is my last incarnation? I have been through so much suffering that I do not want to come back again.

You are not the only person on earth who is miserable. There are billions of people on earth who will say that they are miserable if you ask them. But you are going to come back anyway. God is very clever. He wants His Game to continue and continue. Unless He sees that you are playing the Game extremely well, that is to say, until you have realised Him, God will not allow you to retire. Even after you have realised God, He still may not leave you alone. Still you may have to work.

Again, who am I to say that this is your last incarnation? If I say yes, then difficulties will arise; and if I say no, then you will really feel miserable. So I won't say. Only let us offer our prayer to God to remove suffering from this earth.

If I have to come back to earth in another incarnation, who is going to take care of my soul? If you don't come to this world again, will you name someone else to take care of me?

I will not come back anymore. I have played my role. Once the game is over, you don't play again. When you are playing your part in a game, sometimes you lose the game and sometimes you win. But you will only be concerned that you have played your part. In your case, the most important thing you have to feel is whether or not you have achieved an inseparable oneness with my soul in this incarnation. In the ordinary human life we see the bond between mother and son. You are in Puerto Rico and your son may be in New York. But although you are here working in the office, your heart is inside your son, who may be studying in New York in the university. His heart is also inside you, his mother. From New York the message of all his affection, love and concern is coming to your heart. Even human love, a human bond, has crossed thousands of miles. Your human body will stay on earth for perhaps seventy or eighty years. But in this body you have got something which is called a heart. How it is crossing the distance of thousands of miles! This is your offering and his offering.

In the spiritual plane the teacher himself represents God. His soul is infinitely more illumined than his disciples' souls. But each disciple's soul also wants to be as illumined as the Master's soul.

It is most important for the disciple to establish a real feeling, a radiant feeling of oneness with his Master. If the disciple does not realise God in this incarnation, there will be a definite, direct, express connection between that disciple and his Master. Then in the next incarnation, or in one or two incarnations, the disciple can realise the Highest, the Absolute.

Everybody has to realise God. You may say that you won't eat anything. But there is one thing that you will have to eat, and that is the fruit of the tree of realisation. Other food you may deny, but realisation-food you won't be able to deny. God will say, "All right, if you don't want to eat, don't eat, but this food, the realisation-food, you have to eat sooner or later, in this incarnation or in ten incarnations."

When your master is in the physical, it is the greatest opportunity, because at that time your physical mind is bound to be convinced. When a spiritual Master descends to earth, you get the greatest opportunity. Ramakrishna used to say, "The cow is already there. The cow has milk, but where does the actual milk lie? In the udder. When you milk the cow, you should not try to get milk from the leg of the cow or from the tail of the cow or from the ear of the cow. There is no milk there." So also, divine Bliss is everywhere. But there is a particular time when infinite Grace and Compassion can descend consciously and constantly. And that is when a realised Master descends to earth.

At the end of the game everybody will be judged on where he or she stands in the heart of the Master. Everybody will be given the opportunity; everybody will act; everybody will see the results.

Is it possible for the individual to remember the details of past incarnations?

The soul can easily remember its past incarnations, but it does not want to do so. Let us say that in a past incarnation you were living in Connecticut and now you are living in Puerto Rico. Why should you care to remember every day what your home in Connecticut was like or how many rooms you had there? Your business now is to stay in Puerto Rico in your present house. If anyone asks you where you live, you will say, "I live in Puerto Rico." And if anyone asks you how many rooms you have in your house, you will immediately think of this house and not your previous house.

Please do not pay any attention to the past. Right now you have to do your own work. You have to manifest the qualities that God has given you. You have to do everything here and now. The soul does not care much for the body in which it lived during a previous incarnation. The soul can remember that in a previous incarnation it had better circumstances, surroundings and opportunities. But actually the soul will not care. It just wants to fulfil God in His own way.

You have accepted your fate. You are going to work and study here in Puerto Rico. The soul also feels this way. It says, "Now I am in this body. Let me go on manifesting as much as I can. To think about what I could have done in the past will not solve my problems. Only what I am going to do right now can solve all my problems. "

If you go backward it is a waste of time. Our goal is in front of us, not behind us. The soul does not care at all for the past. It only wants to reach the goal. God-realisation lies ahead of us, not in our past. If we go backwards, we will be wasting our time.

Do all souls have hundreds or thousands of incarnations before realisation?

Yes, it is only spiritual Masters who don't take so many incarnations. There are some exceptions among spiritual Masters, but most of them do not want to go through so many incarnations.

Will the whole world eventually become a better place as a result of the evolution that takes place through reincarnation?

The world is constantly evolving, progressing, consciously or unconsciously. It is like a tiny seed which is sprouting into a plant, and then growing into a tree. There was a time when we were in the mineral world, then in the vegetable world, then in the animal kingdom. Now we are humans; but if we are sincere enough, we will see that although we have a conscious, developed mind, we still have not cast off our animal propensities and qualities. We are still half animals, quarrelling, fighting, struggling. But a day will come when there will be divine people on earth. We will see them just as we are now seeing human beings in front of us.

How can a spiritual Master like yourself convince others who do not believe in reincarnation that it is really true?

If someone asked me to convince him that he had previous lives, even if that individual did not believe in reincarnation, I would be able to prove it to him. I would ask that individual to meditate with me for a few minutes and I would enter into him and bring to the fore his immediate past incarnation. I would bring the image of one or two of his past activities to the fore to such an extent that what he was in his past incarnation would become vivid to the person. I have done it quite a few times in New York. But sometimes it is not right for the person to know his past incarnations, and then I do not tell him.

One of my most devoted disciples one day asked me about his past incarnation. I told him that in his past incarnation he was a boatman in Japan. I told him he could go deep within to see it. I had not even completed my sentence when he himself saw that he was a boatman. But for those who are arrogant, for those who will not believe, and there are people who will not believe when you speak about reincarnation, we have to see if it is worthwhile to convince them about the past. If they are satisfied with their own notion that there is no reincarnation, then let them be satisfied. After all, who is the loser?

A young boy, who was not a disciple of mine, once asked me about his past incarnation. I told him that in his past incarnation he had lived in Germany and had died in an airplane crash. Immediately he said that from the age of three he had been a great admirer of Hitler. He could read German books and German poetry from the age of three. But this information did not help the boy spiritually at all. He was curious and I fed his curiosity, not his spirituality. So in most cases I will not tell a person about his past incarnations.

If somebody lives a good life and reaches Nirvana, does this mean he will not reincarnate again?

Reincarnation does not mean that if somebody does good things, divine things, he will not come back, and if somebody does bad things, wrong things, he will come back. No, everyone will come back into the world, but one who does good things will naturally have a better life in his next incarnation than the one who does bad things.

Nirvana is the path of negation. Those who follow the path of Nirvana want to remain in ultimate Bliss, or you can call it extinction. But we should not use the term "extinction"; it is the ultimate Bliss. These people do not want to reincarnate. When they enter into Nirvana, there the journey ends for them. The soul feels that it will not walk or run further. It does not want to involve itself with earthly activities. Nobody can compel the soul to reincarnate except the Supreme. But although the Supreme has the power to compel the soul, He does not do it. The Supreme does not compel anybody to do anything.

But there are some souls that want to take a conscious part in God's Lila or divine Play. They know that reincarnation is absolutely necessary for those who want to serve God here on earth. One has to realise God on earth; on no other planet or plane can there be any realisation. Then after realisation, some make the promise that they will come back, like Swami Vivekananda and Sri Ramakrishna, who both said that if a single unrealised person remained on earth, then they would be ready to come back.

Can the soul reincarnate in other worlds after death?

The soul that has entered into a human body cannot and does not reincarnate in other worlds. The soul can go through other planes: the physical, vital, mental and psychic sheaths. As soon as the soul leaves the body, it goes through these planes to its own proper region. But there the soul does not reincarnate. The soul is only passing through these places, which are part of its journey of discovery. It is visiting these places, but it does not reincarnate there. The soul reincarnates only in the physical world on earth. Here alone the soul has to manifest its divinity.

There are seven higher worlds and seven lower worlds, and during sleep or meditation everybody's soul travels to these other regions. It may cross through one world after the other going to the highest world; or again, it can go through the lower regions. An ordinary person is not able to see the soul or feel the soul's movements, but a great spiritual aspirant or a spiritual Master can know what the soul is doing and in which plane the soul is. But reincarnation takes place only here on earth, in this world.

Will you please explain how it is that the soul evolves only on the planet Earth?

The soul manifests only on this planet because this planet is in evolution. Evolution means constant progress, constant achievement. When one wants to make progress, when one wants to go beyond, then this is the place. In other worlds, the cosmic gods and other beings are satisfied with what they have already achieved. They do not want to go one inch beyond their achievement. But here on earth you are not satisfied, I am not satisfied, nobody is satisfied with what they have achieved. Dissatisfaction does not mean that we are angry with somebody or angry with the world. No! Dissatisfaction means that we have constant aspiration to go beyond and beyond. If we have only an iota of light, then we want to have more light. Always we want to expand.

When the creation started, the souls took different paths. Those that wanted the ultimate Truth, the infinite Truth, accepted the human body so that they could someday possess, reveal and manifest the Truth here on earth. According to our Indian tradition there are thousands of cosmic gods. There are as many presiding deities and gods as there are human beings. These presiding deities and gods remain in the higher worlds, either in the vital world or in the intuitive world or in some higher plane. Right now, according to their limited capacity, they have more power than we have. But when we are liberated and realised, when we are totally one with the Supreme's Consciousness, with the Supreme's Will, then we shall transcend them.

Our human capacity is infinitely greater than that of the so-called presiding deities because they are satisfied, whereas we are not satisfied with what we have. But actually it is not a case of dissatisfaction; it is a case of constant aspiration. We know that our Supreme Father is infinite. We feel that we have not yet become the Infinite, but we cry to expand, expand. This planet has that inner urge. On the one hand, it is obscure, it is ignorant, it does not care for divine life. But on the other hand, it has that tremendous inner urge of which most human beings are not yet aware. When the inner urge is functioning, then there is no end to our possibilities, no end to our achievements. And when we achieve the Infinite, then naturally we surpass the achievements of other worlds.

Does the soul decide what it is going to go through on the earth plane?

It is the soul that determines what we will do here on earth. But our human mind very often makes friends with ignorance and darkness. So what happens is that some souls have minor difficulties while other souls have great difficulties. The soul has accepted human fate. If the physical mind continues to enter into worldly desires and worldly enjoyments, then naturally the soul will have to fight harder to come out of ignorance. For some time it may be completely covered by ignorance.

But at the same time there are some souls that do not have personal problems. They are very large and wide. That kind of mighty soul feels that all humanity is his family. With all sincerity he takes others' problems upon himself, as if they were his own. These souls are most gracious and most willing to accept and harbour others' sufferings. The great spiritual Masters accept the difficulties of humanity as their very own. If they wanted to be completely separated from humanity, they would not suffer. But they choose to suffer by accepting humanity and they do suffer most intensely for humanity. An ordinary human being who tries to help others who are suffering is himself caught by their suffering. But a realised soul will accept everyone and everything and at the same time he will be flooded with absolute Delight. Even while suffering he has inner Delight because he is constantly one with the Divine, with the Supreme.

In the future, will people always have to aspire like us? Or at some point will people no longer be born on earth?

People will continue to be born and evolution will also continue. We are human beings right now, not animals. But we have so many animal qualities: we quarrel, we fight, we have wars, we do so many undivine things. We actually strangle one another with our hatred and jealousy. But again, we claim that as human beings we are a superior species, we lead a higher life. But in what way? When we enter into ourselves we see that we are human animals. Still, we have made a little progress. We don't want to remain ferocious animals. Among us, some people are really aspiring and crying for God. Eventually they will see the Truth and grow into the Truth. This is evolution.

We cannot say that after four hundred or five hundred years there will be no more animal or human incarnations. There will be animals, there will be people, but they will be more perfect. Now, out of ten thousand people, one person may aspire. But the time will come when it will be just the opposite. We will have made such progress that only one person out of ten thousand will not aspire.

We cannot say that there will be another type of evolution in which everybody will descend fully illumined to earth. No! I have worked hard for centuries in order to realise God. Will someone else not have to work at all? Will God do everything for him immediately? No, everybody has to work. God's Grace descends only when we work hard, when we aspire most soulfully. True, some people realise God when they are in their teens. You may say, "Oh, I have been meditating for twenty or thirty years, while he has meditated only for five or ten years. How is it that he has realised God?" But you do not know that fifty or seventy years ago in his previous incarnation he meditated intensely for many years. Similarly, the world is now imperfect and only gradually, gradually will it become perfect. It is not that at a fixed time the Light will dawn and all unaspiring people will suddenly run toward the Goal. No! Evolution is a slow, gradual process.

How long do we have to continue to reincarnate?

If one aspires, one expedites one's realisation. Otherwise, an ordinary human being takes hundreds and hundreds of incarnations before actual realisation takes place. Aspirants who consciously enter into the path of spirituality and try to discipline themselves on the strength of their inner cry will naturally gain their realisation sooner than those who are still sleeping and are not yet conscious of the inner life.

Now, after one realises God, if it is God's Will, that person need not take any more incarnations. If the person is tired, then he may say, "No, I don't want to be of any help to humanity; I only want to realise God. After realisation I would like to stay in some other plane of consciousness." But some realised souls will want to go back to the earth-consciousness and serve aspiring humanity. It all depends on the individual and on God's Will.

Do the same souls keep coming back to earth?

The same souls do return, but the Supreme also creates new souls. For various reasons many souls have asked to take rest before completing their part in the Cosmic Game. Those who strictly followed the Lord Buddha's path and entered into Nirvana have not come back. So the Supreme sends new souls into the world to take their place.

Will the soul usually look the same throughout its incarnations?

Yes, it will usually remain the same. But inside the soul is the psychic being, which will grow. Once it takes a form, the soul usually stays that way; but the psychic being grows gradually like a small child. At first it is very small, but then it grows up. In spiritual seekers the psychic being is more developed than in other human beings.

Does a beautiful soul always choose a beautiful outer being?

All souls are beautiful in origin. But if a certain soul is a special soul, then naturally in its outer manifestation also we will observe sweetness, beauty, serenity, purity and all other divine qualities. What we are within, we are without.

Some people have very fine souls, wonderful souls, yet in their outer manners they are unfortunately very crude, unlit and uncivilised. Why is this? It is because the mind and the vital have not been properly touched with the soul's light. These individuals do not care for the soul's light and want to remain very crude, so their lives are lacking in harmony. In their outer manifestation they are absolutely unfortunate and miserable.

There is another reason for disharmony between the outer life and the inner life. If we sow the seed of a mango tree, then naturally we will get mangoes. But at times there are other trees around this tree which ruin its beauty. Similarly, if the members of the family do not care for the spiritual life, if they are absolutely unlit, unaspiring, then they can simply crush the finer qualities of a child. How is it that this wonderful child has come into such an undivine family? That is his fate. But generally if one has a beautiful soul, then the outer expression of the soul will also be beautiful.

Does the soul always need physical parents to reincarnate?

Right now the physical body must come from physical parents. But a day will come, most of the spiritual authorities say, when parents will not be required to bring a soul to earth in a physical body. In the occult plane it will be done. And the soul will come into existence with a luminous body. The world is evolving gradually to this point.

I have read that when the soul takes incarnation in the world it is like entering a battlefield. Is this true?

Each time we come back into the field of manifestation and enter into the world, it is like going into a battle. Here the spiritual seeker, the divine soldier, must fight against fear, doubt, anxiety, worry, limitation, bondage and his worst enemy, death. He is constantly fighting against ignorance, and death is the child of ignorance. He fights and then he either loses the battle and dies, or he conquers all these imperfections and negative forces and goes back to God victorious.

When the soul reincarnates in a new body, what happens to the spiritual heart? Does it also go from one lifetime to another like the soul does?

When the soul leaves the body, it takes with it the quintessence of the experiences that the body, mind, vital and heart had in this present life. But when it goes to the soul's region, it does not take the heart or vital or mind with it. Now when it reincarnates in a new body, the soul—or you can say, the psychic being or Purusha —is the same. It still carries the realisations and experiences from its past lives. But it accepts a new heart, new mind, new vital and new body.

When the soul comes back, does it take back the same vital?

It may take either the same one or a vital that is more evolved. It is like buying things in a shop. You leave something in the shop and then you come back and get your own thing or you get something more beautiful. Instead of keeping your old wristwatch, you may buy a new one. And somebody else, who has less money, will like your old one.

Does everybody have a vital and mind that already have been used? Did somebody ever use my vital before, or my heart?

The soul does not care, as long as it has one. It is like a football or any instrument. You use it for a while, and then if you don't like the one you have been using, you will take another one. But if you like a certain ball, you use it again and again until either it is totally destroyed or it gives you total satisfaction. Again, it depends on what the soul wants to accomplish. Sometimes the soul chooses a very powerful mind, and sometimes the soul does not find it necessary. When somebody plays football, if he plays with good players, then he will want to use a good ball. But if one is just going to play with weak players, one can use any kind of ball. So, it depends on whom the soul is going to play with in the battlefield of life.

Why would a soul choose a doubting mind or an aggressive vital?

The soul does not take a doubting mind. The soul accepts the mind, but the very nature of the mind is to doubt.

Would the soul try to get a more illumined mind?

Where is the fun, if all the experts are on one side? Where is the game? The mind is also evolving. When something is in the process of evolution, naturally it takes time to reach its goal. For you, even one day is something. In God's Vision, two hundred years is less than a second; it is nothing. Here on earth, even if the mind is very illumined, earth's consciousness may not be able to receive the mind's light. It is like a pure heart. A pure heart suffers just because it is a pure heart. Why do spiritual people suffer? Because of their heart's magnanimity. There are many people who have a pure heart, but they don't have a strong heart. But if you want to stay on earth, you need a pure heart along with a strong heart.

If the mind makes progress, what happens?

If the mind makes progress, it will try to keep its progress. Then, the next time a soul takes that mind, the mind will be an added help. If a particular mind has got some illumination, that mind will keep it.

Does the mind lose the specific details of its earthly experience?

The mind doesn't need to remember those things. It is like remembering what I ate today, what a disciple's cooking was like. But if I know that that disciple was very kind to me, that she brought me food whenever I wanted it, that is enough. Not how many times she brought food and how many times I liked it; this I do not have to remember. Only her selfless service I shall remember. If the mind wants to know what kind of food she brought, the mind will not be able to know. But it will be able to remember her dedicated service.

What do mental beings do in the mind's world?

Sometimes they sleep, sometimes they inspire, sometimes they enter into human minds and instigate human beings. All of a sudden some thought may come into your mind, and you can't account for it.

When a soul picks a mind or vital, does it already know what kind of life it will have?

It deals with possibility. God knows everything, but He covers up the future. Even God does not use His ultimate Vision all the time; otherwise, there is no game. In forty-five minutes, let us say, the game will be over. God can bring forty-five minutes in front of His Mind immediately. Today, let us say, He will count from one to forty-five, going through each number: one, two, three, four, five, six and so forth. But the next day, if He says "one" and then goes immediately to "forty-five," people will say, "What is the use of playing with You when You can go from one to forty-five immediately and we cannot?" That is why God does not play the game in this way.

When a child incarnates into a family, is it possible that the child's soul is less highly evolved than the parents' souls?

Sometimes the parents are inferior, far inferior to the children, and at other times the parents are superior. But just as in the outer world parents try to make their children wise and well-educated, in the inner world, if parents pray and meditate on their children, the children will make progress and grow.

Does the soul have any choice as to the environment that it will come back to when it reincarnates, and the body that it will take?

Nobody imposes on the soul. The soul itself makes the choice, but it has to be approved by the Supreme. The soul, while sitting at the top of the tree, feels that if it comes down to earth, it will be able to fulfil itself. But, as you know, the world is full of imperfections and limitations. And when the soul touches the foot of the tree, it feels that there are all unlit forces, evil forces, trying to capture and devour it. So after making the choice, sometimes the soul feels that the environment it has chosen is unhealthy, and it may leave the body.

You said that the soul chooses the family in which it is going to be born. What happens to the soul if it chooses a bad family?

Let us take the soul as the owner of the house and the family as the house. As the owner, if you feel that this particular house is not giving you joy or not fulfilling you, then immediately you will try to get another which will give you fulfilment. When the soul is disgusted with a particular family, it may leave its present body and enter into some other body. Since the soul has wisdom and light, it will come back in a place with a better environment, one that offers more fulfilment. If the house is all right, then the soul does not have to move. When you have a nice house, you do not want to change it; you want to get as much as possible from that house. When the soul gets a proper house, that is to say a good environment and a good family in which everyone is aspiring, then naturally the soul will stay there.

Do a person's relatives in this incarnation have any connection with his relatives in a past incarnation?

It depends on God's Will. Your grandfather in this incarnation may not want to keep any connection with your family, so in his next incarnation he will enter into some other family. Sometimes souls try to change the game. They do not want to continue the same game. One soul will say, "I have played my part. Now I want to have a connection with another family." Again, someone may be your grandfather in this incarnation, but if he wants to remain in the same family he can come back to you in another incarnation as your grandson. Naturally he will come in a different form, as a grandson, a nephew or cousin. In the same way the mother can come as a daughter, a cousin or a sister. So there is no hard and fast rule.

Did any of your disciples know each other in past incarnations?

This is not our first and this cannot be our last incarnation. Previously I used to speak much about past incarnations, but recently I have stopped because it only creates confusion. On rare occasions when the Supreme tells me to make disciples aware of their past incarnations, I do so. When the Supreme asks me to do it, that means it is going to help the persons concerned and also others who are present.

There are two disciples here who are close friends in this incarnation. When I was meditating on them, I saw that they were physical brothers in their previous incarnation and were very close to each other. In their last incarnation, they had two more brothers, and in this incarnation they will see them. When the other brothers come to me, I shall show them both to you. I cannot say that all four brothers will stay with me as disciples all of this life. But when they come, I will definitely be able to show these friends that they were brothers in the past. I believe the last two brothers are going to come in six or seven months' time. Either these two friends will bring them or they will come in some other way. Then it will be up to them to follow my path or not.

The past doesn't end with this. In their previous incarnation the two friends here were brothers, but prior to that, they were son and father. Nothing can eclipse my third eye's vision. I see that one was the father and one was the son. In this incarnation, the father and the son, the two brothers, have come to my path. In this incarnation both of them will also be one on the spiritual level. Human brothers and human fathers and sons come and go. But when you have established real spiritual oneness, that feeling cannot disappear. When a spiritual father unites two spiritual brothers, they are bound forever. When I say that they are bound, that doesn't mean that they will be so completely bound that they want to kill each other. No. They will only have the feeling of true inseparable oneness. Both will help each other immensely.

Indeed, it is a great joy to see the members of our family coming back to us from past incarnations. In this incarnation if the relationship is based on spirituality, then the members can really help each other considerably. However, if one is following the spiritual path and the other is following an ordinary path, it is usually hopeless. The spiritual one will think the other is still in ignorance, and the one who is leading an ordinary life will think that the spiritual one is of no use because he has given up the world. They will misunderstand each other. But if both follow the spiritual life, it is a real divine blessing.

If the dear ones, the brothers and sisters, come back again together and they are conscious of what they were, that does help them make real progress. Their progress will be very fast because they will get some benefit from the past. I always say that the past is dust. Yes, the past did not give the disciples realisation, but if in the past they had a feeling of oneness or closeness with someone, then when they learn of their past association, they recover that closeness and that oneness. It is not actually the past, but only the disciples' sense of oneness, only their larger self, that I am bringing back into the disciples' own consciousness.

What is the relationship of the individual soul to the soul of the country that it is born into?

There are many countries. Why does a particular soul enter into a particular country? There are two basic reasons: either the soul has been commanded by the Supreme or the soul has a specific preference for that country. Why will a soul care for a particular country? It is because the soul has its own inner propensities. It feels that it has some inner intuitive capacity or other quality which can be easily brought into manifestation if it takes incarnation in a particular country. If a particular soul has dynamism, it will try to take incarnation in America, not India. Again, if it cries for inner harmony and peace, then it will try to take incarnation in India. If the soul wants vastness and a combination of mind and heart in mental and psychic awakening, then it will incarnate in Australia.

The individual soul may want a particular country, and at the same time the soul of a country also wants a particular type of soul, so that its own reality can be manifested. Each soul has something special to offer to its country. So, the soul of each country meditates upon the highest Reality to get souls which will be of help to it.

If the soul likes a specific country, the Supreme can accept or reject the soul's choice. But ninety-nine times out of a hundred the Supreme approves the soul's choice. However, if the Supreme makes the choice, then usually the individual soul cannot alter the Supreme's Will. Again, just as we sometimes do not listen to our boss, the soul also may do this. But usually the individual soul listens to the Supreme because souls have more light than earthbound beings.

Each individual soul has a special role to play in the country that is accepting it. But once it plays its role, its goes to another country. Of course, the soul can have two or three incarnations in a particular country and then go to another place. Again, some souls may want to take more incarnations in a particular place.

What is the role that the individual soul plays? It is the role of a flower on a tree. When there are many flowers on a tree, then the tree looks beautiful. Each soul is like a flower and each country is like a tree.

When does the soul enter the body?

Between six and eight months before birth is the usual time for the soul to enter into the body. On rare occasions it may enter at the time of conception. The latest time for the soul to enter is usually about thirteen or fourteen days before the child is born. In very rare cases the soul enters into the body just two or three days before birth and sometimes it may even come shortly after birth. At that time the soul may be waiting until the last moment before making a decision because it is doubtful about the family. Some souls feel that by waiting for a longer time they will be able to make a better decision. Again, some souls simply take longer to make the decision just as some people take more time to make a decision than others. But some souls don't wait; they know immediately what to do and it is done within a few months after the time of conception.

What does the soul do in the body before birth?

The soul remains absolutely silent in the body. It is like a witness. It just observes the physical organs. But what it sees when it comes into the world for the first time at birth will give it a kind of fear and frustration. The soul is a spark of the Divine, but when it enters into the world, immediately it sees ignorance. The soul has accepted the world, but the moment the child is born, the soul sees through the eyes of the child and what it sees creates fear within the soul. The soul at that time does not see anything wonderful; it sees something ferocious like a lion that wants to devour it. Then the soul says: "It is I who have taken this body. I have to fight. Why should I act like a coward? Why should I leave the body? In this body, with this body, I shall have to fight for God and establish His Kingdom here on earth."

Is the soul always assured that it will find its true mission during each new lifetime on earth?

Before taking human incarnation, the soul gets the inner message about its divine purpose on earth. It is fully conscious of its mission and it comes here with the direct approval or sanction of the Supreme. But during the lifetime, the workings of the physical mind sometimes cover up the divine inspiration and the true purpose of the soul. Then the mission of the soul cannot come forward. However, if we start aspiring with the mind, the heart and the soul, then we can learn the purpose of our existence here on earth.

There is a constant battle going on between the divine and undivine in each human being. The ignorance of the world tries to devour human aspiration. At the present stage of evolution, most human beings live in the undivine vital, where all is desire, anxiety and excitement. That is why they are unconscious of the soul's needs.

Is it predestined how far the soul will progress in an incarnation?

In some cases it is predestined and in some cases there is no fixed limit; it depends on how much Grace the soul receives.

Can you help me to leave the body as soon as possible, and help me to reincarnate in a place that is high and very cold, with plenty of fog and snow?

I have the power to do what you are asking me. But if I go to the Supreme with your petition, immediately He will laugh at me and say, "What kind of disciple do you have who, when he is just starting to open his eyes, wants to close them again?" Climate has nothing to do with God-realisation. Sri Ramana Maharshi and Sri Aurobindo were from South India, which has a very hot climate, but this did not prevent them from realising God. There are many aspirants living in caves far up in the Himalayas, in the eternal snows, who have not been able to realise God. The climate has nothing to do with it. It is the inner heat of aspiration that can bring God-realisation, not outer climate conditions.

Tagore, our greatest poet, used to write six or eight poems daily. He once thought that if he could retire to a solitary place he could write much better poetry. So he left his house and confined himself to a solitary place in the mountains. While there, he was not able to write a single piece of poetry. He discovered that it is not the environment that is most important, but the inner inspiration. God has chosen the conditions under which you are living your present life. It is like a play. The stage is set and the curtain has been raised for you to perform your part and advance along the spiritual path. Your present conditions are the best possible ones for your advancement. Now you want to leave the body and enter into a new body in a future incarnation so you can have an environment that you think will suit you best. But this kind of life would be worse than your present one because it is chosen by your mind, whereas your present life was chosen by God.

If your past actions of this incarnation are bothering you, I wish to tell you that my philosophy is "The past is dust." Whatever you did a few years ago or even yesterday should not concern you. The past is not important. It is what you do from now on that can expedite your progress. Now you have a spiritual Master in a physical body to help you. And it is the present, and the future flowing into the present, that can give you liberation.

Is all suffering the result of bad karma, either from this life or from a past life?

Not necessarily. Sometimes what happens is that even though we have not done anything wrong, our soul wants to have an experience of suffering. Our soul wants to enter into the depth of pain just to know what pain is. Suppose a very spiritual person finds it necessary to thrash another person. What does he do? Immediately he enters into the person whom he is beating and identifies with him. And the intensity with which he feels this experience is much more than that of the person who is actually being beaten.

Many times we do wrong things and we get the results sooner or later. But again, there are times when we suffer because of the cosmic forces. Sometimes sincere, very devoted parents have children who are absolutely unspiritual, undivine and worthless. Now you will say that perhaps in their past incarnation the parents were also unspiritual and did many wrong things. In some cases the parents were bad in their previous lives, but in other cases this may not be true. Sometimes sincere seekers are affected by hostile, animal-like forces that are operating in the world. When these undivine, hostile forces that are hovering around behave like mad elephants or enter into a person, then the person suffers. It is like this: around us are animals fighting, quarrelling and destroying each other. A mad elephant, no matter how nice and sincere you are, will simply destroy you. You never know when these animals are moving around. So when a sincere seeker suffers, we cannot immediately come to the conclusion that in his past incarnation he did something wrong.

If we follow the spiritual life all the time, then we stay in the field of divine Power, which is like a fort. We are inside the fort being protected by God. When wrong forces, undivine forces, try to attack us, the divine Grace stands in their way. Spiritual people try always to be conscious of God's Compassion, God's Blessing and God's Light, because they know that even if they do not do wrong things, they may be attacked by undivine forces. And when they do wrong things, immediately they know that there is someone who can forgive them, who can protect them, who can elevate their consciousness, and this someone is their Inner Pilot, or God.

Could you please explain how the law of karma affects us in this life and our next life?

We are carrying the past inside us. It is a continuous flow. "As you sow, so you reap." If we do something wrong, we have to know that either today or tomorrow, either in the physical world or in the inner world, we will get the result. If I constantly steal, one day I will be caught and put into jail. I may not get caught today, but one day I will be caught. And if I do something good, if I pray, if I meditate and do divine things, I will get the result of this also. Sometimes we see someone who has done something wrong enjoying the world. But perhaps he did something extraordinary, something wonderful in his immediate past incarnation, and now he is having the result of his good action, while the results of his bad deeds have not yet started to bear fruit. In the evening of his life, or in a future life, he will definitely be punished.

In the case of an ordinary, unaspiring person, karmic dispensation is unavoidable, inevitable. The law of karma is always binding; like a snake it will coil around him. He has to pay the toll, the tax; the law of karma is merciless. But again, there is something called divine Grace. I was ignorant and I did a few things wrong. But if I shed bitter tears and cry for forgiveness, then naturally God's Compassion will dawn on me. When a person enters into the spiritual life, his karma can easily be nullified if it is the Will of God operating through a spiritual Master. Slowly God's infinite Grace can nullify the results of his bad karma and expedite the results of his good karma. If a seeker not only wants the spiritual life but also sincerely practises the spiritual life every day, then he can stand above the law of karma, for God is bound to shower His boundless Grace on the devoted head and heart of the aspirant. Of course, I cannot go on doing some undivine thing and feel that God will always forgive me. No. But if God sees a soulful cry looming large from within, if He sees that I am sincere and aspiring and want to be free from the meshes of ignorance, He will not only forgive me but He will also give me the necessary strength not to make the same mistake again.

When we come back in our next incarnation, naturally we have to start our journey according to the result of our past karma. If we have done many things wrong, we cannot expect to realise the highest Truth in our next incarnation. But if God's Grace is there, we can easily nullify the wrong things we have already done during this life.

How can I get rid of bad karma?

It depends on whether it comes from this incarnation or past incarnations. Sometimes a person will say, "In my past incarnation I did many wrong things." But it may be due to circumstance: your husband or son did something wrong in the past. You have to know that the law of karma is very complicated. Many times an individual gets punishment from association, because he is a member of a certain family. You may say that the very fact that he is in that particular family is karma. Otherwise, why did he come into that family? There is a great difference between karma you have accrued and karma caused by others. So, in your case, please tell me, is it your own karma or others' bad karma from which you are suffering?

I think it is my karma.

Is it from this incarnation or the past?

This incarnation.

In this incarnation you feel that you have done a few things wrong and now you are suffering. If you have done something wrong, then you know about it and God knows about it.

Others also know that you have done something wrong, but they cannot rectify your mistake. Only God can help. If you go deep within, God will tell you that your wrong karma is just an experience and that now that experience is over. You have done something wrong and have suffered. That experience was written in God's Heart, and now it is deleted. The moment you suffered, your bad karma entered into God's Cosmic Flow.

The voice of silence within you tells you to feel that you did something wrong and that you have offered the experience to God. So now you are in no way responsible. Whenever you do something wrong, act like a child. Whenever a child does something wrong, he runs to his mother. He knows that his mother will protect him. The soul is like a mother. The soul will protect you and give you wisdom. If you know you have done something wrong, immediately run to your Eternal Mother, the soul inside you. Then the law of karma will not affect you, because the soul has more power than the mistakes that you have committed. The soul gets that power from the Supreme. Even if you have suffered and are afraid that your suffering will come back, you will not suffer if you run towards the soul. In this way the law of karma can be nullified.

If a disciple does not realise God while his Guru is in the body, how would the Guru be able to help the disciple in that person's next incarnation if there were no other living Guru through whom he could work?

The Guru does not need another Guru to work through. Four thousand years ago Lord Krishna had disciples when he was actually on earth, and even now there are still many of his disciples who have not accepted another Master. They reincarnate, for instance, into a family which is following the path of Krishna, so that Krishna will be able to give them liberation in his own way. It is similar with the other great Masters. There are many of Ramakrishna's disciples who have come back to earth. They have not gone to any other Guru, yet they are being fulfilled. But if they wanted another Master, Ramakrishna would naturally tell them to go to another one. Some disciples of great Masters have accepted other Gurus. Some of my own disciples, in fact, were with Lord Krishna.

How can a spiritual Master help his disciples if they do not go to some other Guru? He can do it through his conscious will, his soul's will. I am here on earth, and although I am not in England or Puerto Rico, through my conscious will, early in the morning after 2 a.m. I concentrate on all those who are my disciples there. To concentrate for a fleeting second is enough, but I use more than that to know what the soul is doing, and how far the soul has gone. So even while remaining in the physical, which is real bondage, a spiritual Master can help his disciples in different parts of the world. Then when he leaves the body, he is totally free. From the other shore the spiritual Master works through the soul's light or will-power. The soul's light can be offered from any plane of consciousness, from the highest plane right down to the earth plane. So from the higher worlds the Master can easily connect with the disciple's aspiring soul, and the disciple can respond to the Master's light. It is in this way that the Master can and does and must help the disciple.

When a Master accepts someone as a real disciple, a true disciple, he makes a promise to God, the Supreme, and to the soul of the individual seeker that he will be eternally responsible for that soul. But there are many, many who will come to our path—hundreds of thousands. They may stay with me for ten, twenty, thirty or even forty years, but never really accept me. When a Master leaves the body, he is not responsible for these so-called disciples. The Master will leave them to their own fate.

Now some may say, "How is it that we have been coming to the Centre and you have not accepted us as true disciples?" The simple reason is that they have not accepted me wholeheartedly. Only someone who has really accepted our path can be considered a real disciple. Acceptance has to be mutual; nobody can force it. Human parents force, but a spiritual Master cannot.

Outwardly I have not personally told all those who are my real disciples, but inwardly I have told them, and they can rest assured that when I leave the body they will not be lost. They will never be lost, either in this

incarnation or in their future incarnations. The real disciples—those who have taken me as their own and
whom I have taken as my very own—are going to be fulfilled and realised in this incarnation or in their next
incarnation or in very few incarnations. Some disciples
may take twenty incarnations or more because of their
very poor start. Some who have come to me in their first
or second human incarnation may take hundreds of
incarnations. The first or second human incarnation is a
half-animal incarnation. The animal is still there as the
predominating factor, so how can they achieve God-
realisation? Even in the New York Centre there are
many disciples who have had only six or seven human
incarnations.

When great Masters come to earth they greatly expedite the progress of their disciples. But how far can they
expedite it when the disciples themselves have made so
little headway? Still, the Masters make a very brave
fight; they challenge ignorance. They say: "Let us see
how far we can go." Again, some disciples who have
been on earth for only a few incarnations may run the
fastest because of their sincerity, humility and eagerness
to run. They do not use their previous obscure qualities,
and their mind has not been covered by millions of
thoughts and ideas. From the very beginning of their
spiritual life they start marching. They come into a spiritual family, or if they are fortunate enough, something
pushes them forward from within to come to the Light.
There is something called divine fortune. Some people
have that fortune, and if they utilise it in a proper way,
then everything is possible in one incarnation. Otherwise, it takes hundreds of years.

How will you keep contact with us after you leave the body?

I will have a special telephone with telephone operators. There *is* one. Let me tell you a very charming incident. In India in 1951 or so, I was sitting beside my friend Jyotish outside the house. Jyotish was very dear to me, so it was only for him that I did this. He wanted to get some messages from his mother, who had died seven or eight years previously.

I said, "Look here, I am using my telephone. Now I am going to bring a message from you to your mother. Then I will get a message from her and it will come to you directly as the answer. I will ask your mother a question on your behalf, but the answer you will get." I asked three questions. The answers came and he received them, and he was deeply moved. First I sent his soul and then my soul to his mother's soul. Then they had a conversation and from there he got the messages.

Now when Jyotish was about twenty-five years old, five ladies fell in love with him, but he never married any of them. Because of their previous karma, they all died together in a boat accident. He was in Burma at the time of the accident. So these five ladies were also in the soul's world with his mother.

When I told him that I would bring a message from his girlfriends too, he said, "How will you know who they are if I don't tell you their names?" I said to him, "I will enter through your soul and I will bring you their names. Now in silence you repeat the names of the girls. From each I will ask a question and you will get the answer." He was so clever; he thought he would trick me. For three he thought of the real names, but for the other two he thought of totally false names. I was about to say

121

these false names when immediately his soul stood in front of me and told me the truth. His soul protected me. I said, "Oh, you are trying to deceive me with these last two names!" and he fell flat at my feet.

Then the ashram gossip started. From where to where we descended on that day! The next day Jyotish told a close mutual friend about this experience and asked, "Do you believe it?" The friend said, "Perhaps you were drunk. He is always drunk. Only drunkards can do this kind of thing! By knowing about your friends, what benefit do you get?" Inwardly the friend believed it, but outwardly he pretended not to.

When one disciple of mine died, I told his small nephews that we could talk to their uncle in the soul's world, just like on a telephone. I thought of doing a little of this for them, but my inner being warned me that they would be frightened, terribly frightened, and it would create problems, so I did not do it.

If one is a spiritual person, will his next incarnation be different from that of an ordinary person?

Certainly. If a soul is very spiritually advanced, it will not take an ordinary life, because it will have already gone through the ordinary life. Each incarnation is a steppingstone towards our ultimate God-realisation. When one has consciously aspired in his last incarnation, his future birth will hold more opportunities for his spiritual progress. Now if a seeker actually started his spiritual life in his past incarnation, if he was really sincere in his spiritual practices in his previous life, then naturally in this life he will start aspiring at a very young age. He will be born into a spiritual family where he will be encouraged to lead the spiritual life from his very birth, and he will start aspiring when he is ten or twelve or fourteen or sixteen. It may happen, however, that his circumstances are bad. Then even if he had started his spiritual life in his past incarnation, in this incarnation he will go slowly because he will not get help from his parents or from his environment. But it is not a risk; it is a journey. In the process of evolution the soul covers thousands of inner miles gaining different experiences, and it is these experiences that eventually give the soul its fullest realisation.

But if the person was a very great aspirant who was about to realise God, then he will almost definitely come into a very highly developed spiritual family, and from the very beginning he will be able to enter into the true spiritual life. Most of the real spiritual Masters enter into very highly developed spiritual families. God may send a spiritual Master into an unaspiring family, since He is not bound by any plan, but in most cases spiritual Masters come into spiritual families.

You said before that each incarnation is a stepping-stone towards our God-realisation. Does that mean that we can't reach God in this life?

No, not at all. It is a matter of previous background and aspiration. If one has been aspiring and meditating in previous lifetimes, then there is no reason why he cannot attain realisation in his present incarnation on the strength of his aspiration. Since we are all progressing towards realisation, in one incarnation or another this realisation is bound to take place. As I said, it is a matter of the aspirant's spiritual development.

If a seeker dies, do all his responsibilities and work cease in the period between his death and his rebirth? Or is he able to work consciously, or in some way continue the work that he started, before he comes back to earth?

It depends on the achievement of the individual seeker. Suppose an advanced seeker has left the body, and suppose there were many things he had wanted to accomplish on earth when he was here, but he could not. What will he do? When he leaves the body, he has to go through the physical sheath, vital sheath, mental sheath and other sheaths, and then he will enter into the soul's region. If it is not his own will to come back to the earth for ten or twenty years, and if it is also not God's Will for him to come back, then in the meantime he can get his work done on earth through someone still on earth who is dearest to him. Because he is an advanced soul, he can apply his soul's will from where he is to his dearest one on earth. But ordinary human beings cannot do this when they leave the body.

Say, for example, someone wants his children to get their master's degree. Then after leaving the body, as long as the soul is in the vital world, in the subtle sheath, it can send these desires and ordinary wishes to the children. Through the vital, the soul still keeps some physical contact with earth. Ordinary earthly desires can be fulfilled or enhanced by the will of the deceased person who has left the body a year or two earlier.

But when the soul goes back to the higher planes, at that time it will not desire, it will not operate in this way on sons or daughters who are still on earth. The soul will not care for the children's earthly satisfaction, for the fulfilment of their teeming earthly desires. But if the soul has Heavenly aspiration for its dear ones, from the higher worlds it will try to increase their aspiration and help them in every possible way. The soul will go to mighty souls who are still on earth and beg them to help the dear ones in the spiritual world. But if the soul is very highly evolved and it sees that somebody is really sincere and aspiring, then the soul itself can help that person.

When someone dies, in his next incarnation does he maintain the same level of aspiration?

When someone dies, in his next incarnation he definitely maintains the same level of aspiration within his new body and new consciousness. But this aspiration usually cannot come to the fore because the earth-consciousness is full of darkness and ignorance. He has to fight against tremendous opposition for a few years or, in most cases, quite a number of years. But again, if the soul is most powerful, if the seeker himself has unusual inner strength, then either from the very dawn of his life or in a few years' time he regains his old aspiration and continues to march and run towards his destined Goal.

Is the length of time the soul remains in the soul's world between incarnations determined by the aspiration of the previous incarnation? If it is an elevated soul, will it incarnate sooner?

It is according to the aspiration and according to the necessity. You may have the aspiration to do something, but at the same time God may not feel the necessity for you to do it. From your side aspiration is necessary. You are aspiring to come back again and to start the game again immediately. It is as if you have played for half an hour and now you are taking a short rest. Then, if you do not want to rest any longer, you say: "Give me the opportunity to finish the game and go back." But God may say, "No, I want you to take rest for a while longer." At that time you cannot return. But if your aspiration and God's necessity become one, then certainly you can come back.

Some souls reincarnate almost immediately, without even going to the soul's region. Suppose somebody dies prematurely in an accident. At that time his soul may go only up to the vital sheath and from there, if a spiritual figure or the divine Grace intervenes, in seven or eight months it will take incarnation in a new family.

Most ordinary souls come back again after staying in the soul's world for six or seven or, at most, twenty years. The time in the soul's world is used by the soul to assimilate its experiences on earth. Great people, such as great scientists or spiritual figures, do not take birth again as rapidly as ordinary people. Very rarely will you see a great figure in any field who will take incarnation again very soon. Some stay in the soul's world for seventy years or more. In certain cases, spiritual Masters wait a hundred or two hundred years before reincarnating. But there is no hard and fast rule. If the Supreme wants them to come back to earth, they have to come back even if they do not want to. It is the soul's own decision, plus the approval of the Supreme, that determines how long it takes for a person to reincarnate.

If someone is gifted in one area, does this mean that his soul was originally given this potentiality, or did he try to achieve this for many lives and then finally achieve it?

Potentiality everybody has, like a lump of clay. When one potter shapes it, the pot becomes most beautiful, and another potter makes a pot that is not so beautiful. The essence of both pots is the same—clay. Likewise, in spirit we are all one. But while the one potter is moulding, you may ask, "Why has he moulded that particular pot so attractively?" There is something in that particular potter that is called conscious aspiration. In every other respect my essence, your essence, everybody's essence remains the same. But while that particular potter is moulding, there is something inside him which gives him the opportunity to make something unique.

So it is not that right from the beginning a particular potentiality was given. No, it was destined for each person to receive very limited freedom, which started right from the beginning of creation. Now this freedom means potential. Some use this potential for the spiritual life, some use it for music, some for poetry and so on. Some do not use it at all. But potentiality will not develop into reality unless and until it is brought to the fore and developed by its possessor.

Do the physical abilities we possess have anything to do with our achievements in our previous incarnations?

No, our physical abilities depend on how much determination, perseverance and aspiration we have. If we have very few abilities, it does not mean that we were undivine in our previous incarnations. No, it is only that some people don't try; they don't work hard. In this world nothing can be achieved without working very hard for it.

According to reincarnation, our next life is supposed to be a reflection and extension of this life. Could you please elaborate on this?

Our next life need not be a reflection of the previous life. Suppose somebody has played his role most satisfactorily. Suppose you were a great artist in your previous incarnation and your soul does not want to have that experience again. If your soul wants you to have the experience of being a politician, then your previous experience as an artist may not come to the fore at all. If the soul has not completed its role in a specific field and wants to continue the same process, only then will one life be a reflection of the previous life. Otherwise, the soul may change the characteristics, nature and propensities of the human being totally.

Sometimes my cousin and I meditate by looking into each other's eyes, and when we do sometimes we see one another's faces change and even the hair turns a different colour. I was wondering what this means.

You are seeing his past incarnation and he is seeing yours. But this is not at all advisable. Suppose you see that three or four incarnations ago you were an animal, even though you had a human body. There are many people like this. If we do not pray or meditate, then here on earth we are little better than animals. In Jamaica, in Puerto Rico, in Canada, in New York, when I walk along the street I see people who have incarnated as human beings for the first time. What can you expect from them? They have just come from the animal kingdom.

For two disciples to look at each other and consciously concentrate on the eyes and bring forward the past is very risky, for you may be unconsciously bringing forward your animal consciousness. In India I know people who have done this with their brothers and sisters, and then the undivine forces from the past incarnation of one have entered into the other, and vice versa. Even in this incarnation, as long as we have not realised God, there are many undivine elements in our nature which we have to contend with. So let us not bring forward the past. This past, I always say, is dust. Has the past given you realisation? No! If it had, then you would not have come to me. So it is not necessary or advisable to go to the past.

Does it help you to know what kind of animal you were in your past incarnations, or what kind of person you were?

When we enter into the inner life and develop our inner consciousness, our inner capacity, we get reminiscences of our past incarnations. Deep in our meditation we can easily feel that we had previous lives. And if we know that we had a past, and if we know that the present is not yet complete and that we ourselves can never remain incomplete, then the urge of the present will take us to the future where we will achieve our completeness. At the same time, we can expedite our progress if we have a Master. If we are most dedicated to the inner life and if we have a Guru, then we can make twenty incarnations' progress in one lifetime.

Now suppose we know that we were a deer in our last animal incarnation. The only advantage is that we can think of our speed and say: "In the animal incarnation I ran so fast, and at that time I did not have the advanced soul which I now have. In this incarnation let me run even faster!" As soon as we remember that we ran fast in a previous incarnation, we feel inspired to run fast in this incarnation. If we know our past incarnation, then we can utilise it positively; at that time inspiration comes forward very quickly. If somebody knows that he was a seeker, then he gets a little joy and confidence. "I started my journey in my past incarnation, but it was a very long and arduous road. In this incarnation I am still walking along the same path, but I don't have as far to go this time. Also, it is easier because I have a little help. I have the capacity. I have the willingness. I have the experience. With a spiritual Master guiding me, I shall easily reach my goal."

But only on very rare occasions do we utilise knowledge of our past incarnations properly. Most of the time it does not give us any encouragement at all. If we know that in our past incarnation we were a thief or something undivine, will this give us any inspiration or aspiration? No! Immediately we will think: "Oh, I was a thief and in this incarnation I am trying to become a saint. Impossible! It is hopeless to try to become spiritual in this life." Even in this incarnation if we do a few things wrong it takes us a long time to come out of despair. We think: "I was so bad. I did this. I did that. Now how am I going to become pure? How am I going to realise God?" Even if we did something wrong four years ago it may still bother us.

On the other hand, suppose we know that in our past incarnation we were someone very great and in this incarnation we see that we are nothing. Then we will feel miserable. We will curse God and we will curse ourselves. We will say: "If I was so great, how is it that in this incarnation I am so useless? What unthinkable thing have I done to deserve this fate? God is harsh; He does not care for me." But we misunderstand God. God wants to have a different experience through us in this incarnation, and we think that God is just being unkind.

An aspirant wants inner joy, the joy that fulfils him and fulfils God. This he will never get from his past incarnations. If he enters into some past incarnation and sees that he was the President of the United States, still he will get no satisfaction. He will see that as President his life was full of misery, frustration and all kinds of suffering. For real joy, an aspirant has to go forward in the spiritual life with his own aspiration and inner cry, with his own concentration and meditation.

The best thing for us is not to think of the past. Our goal is not behind us; it is ahead of us. Our direction is forward, not backward. For a spiritual person I always say: "The past is dust." I say this because the past has not given us what we want. What we want is God-realisation. Knowing our previous incarnations does not help our God-realisation. God-realisation depends entirely on our inner cry. The important thing is not the past, but the present. We must say: "I have no past. I am beginning here and now with God's Grace and my own aspiration. Now let me start to run. How far I have run in the past is immaterial. Let me think only of how far I am going to run in this life."

Right now we see the past as something totally different from the present, and the present as something totally different from the future. Once we realise God, at that time the past, present and future become all one. They form a circle, which is our own inner being, our entire life. At that time we can easily see back to our previous incarnations and know what we were.

If you want to know about your past incarnations, certainly God will give you the capacity. But the most important thing is not past incarnations or future incarnations, but what you want here and now. You want God, and if you meditate soulfully, God is bound to grant you that boon. You will possess Him and you will claim Him as your very own.

I wish to say one more thing to my disciples. Now let me brag a little, and you also can boast. In your past incarnations you did lead spiritual lives. If you had not had any preparation, do you think that God would have brought you to me? No! He would have taken you to some Master who is an inch lower than me. Spiritual Masters of my calibre get disciples who have tried or done something in the past. Some have done more, some have done less. But everybody has done something; otherwise you would have gone to some other spiritual Master and not to me. God is kind to me and He is kind to you. To the high school teacher God will not give kindergarten students. He will save kindergarten students for those who cannot teach higher classes. On rare occasions, one or two have come to me after only a few human incarnations, but these few souls have an intense desire to transcend their present consciousness.

If a person is a very advanced seeker and develops the ability to see his past incarnations, will this actually hinder his progress? In other words, is it always harmful if you discover you were a thief or something in the past?

If you are meditating most sincerely in this life, your inner strength will automatically develop and you will reach the point where you will not be disturbed even if you see that you were the worst possible criminal in a previous incarnation. You know that you have come here to transform yourself, to go towards the Divine. The Lord Buddha disclosed his previous incarnations: he was a goat and many other things. But because he had realised God and had entered into the highest Truth, it was easy for him to say what he was in his previous births. To him it was immaterial if he was most ordinary in his previous incarnations.

If a man dies and he is very fond of a dog or other animal, and if he has compassion for that animal, will this cause him to reincarnate as an animal? I understand that in India while a great sage was meditating in the woods something happened to a small lamb. He took care of it and became very fond of it and, as a result, in his next incarnation he was a lamb.

The greatest scripture in India and the largest in the world is called the Mahabharata. In the Mahabharata there are quite a few stories in which a man later reincarnates as an animal. There is a famous story about a king named Bharata, who was very fond of deer and who supposedly became a deer in his next incarnation.

Now Ramakrishna, the great spiritual Master, was very fond of Swami Vivekananda, his dearest disciple. He used to seek out the disciple and talk to him, and people thought that Ramakrishna was mad. So one day Vivekananda said to him: "What are you doing? Don't you know the story of King Bharata who was so attached to a deer that he became a deer in his next incarnation? So your fate is also going to be like that, if you constantly think of an ordinary human being like me." Ramakrishna took Vivekananda seriously, and asked Mother Kali: "Is this true that my fate will be also like that of King Bharata?" She said: "That is stupid! You are fond of Naren [Vivekananda] because you are seeing God in him. It is not because he is beautiful or something else. No! You are fond of him because the manifestation of God is expressed in him. That is why you are so delighted when you see him."

So if you show compassion to someone, that does not mean that you are going to become that person. If a beggar comes to you for alms and you show your utmost compassion to the beggar and give him some money or food, it doesn't mean that you are going to become a beggar yourself. Similarly, if you have a dog, you can show your love for the dog because it is extremely faithful to you and so on. But this does not mean that you will become a dog because you admire the qualities of the dog that you love. The good qualities that the dog has, the faithfulness the dog has, you can have in your human existence, without taking an animal life. Just by showing attachment to an animal you are not going to become an animal. You have already passed through that stage. What you get is the good qualities of the animal.

About the Author

SRI CHINMOY is a fully realised spiritual Master dedicated to inspiring and serving those seeking a deeper meaning in life. Through teaching of meditation, his music, art and writings, his athletics and his own life of dedicated service to humanity, he tries to show others how to find inner peace and fulfilment.

Born in Bengal in 1931, Sri Chinmoy entered an ashram (spiritual community) at the age of 12. His life of intense spiritual practice included meditating for up to 14 hours a day, together with writing poetry, essays and devotional songs, doing selfless service and practising athletics. While still in his early teens, he had many profound inner experiences and attained spiritual realisation. He remained in the ashram for 20 years, deepening and expanding his realisation, and in 1964 came to New York City to share his inner wealth with sincere seekers.

Today, Sri Chinmoy serves as a spiritual guide to disciples in some 100 centres around the world. He advocates the "Path of the Heart," as the simplest way to make rapid spiritual progress. By meditating on the spiritual heart, he teaches, the seeker can discover his own inner treasures of peace, joy, light and love. The role of a spiritual Master, according to Sri Chinmoy, is to help the seeker live so that these inner riches can illumine his life. He instructs his disciples in the inner life and elevates their consciousness not only beyond their expectation, but even beyond their imagination. In return he asks his students to meditate regularly and to try to nurture the inner qualities he brings to the fore in them.

Sri Chinmoy teaches that love is the most direct way for a seeker to approach the Supreme. When a child feels love for his father, it does not matter how great the father is in the world's eye; through his love the child feels only his oneness with his father and his father's possessions. This same approach, applied to the Supreme, permits the seeker to feel that the Supreme and His own Eternity, Infinity and Immortality are the seeker's own. This philosophy of love expresses the deepest bond between man and God, who are aspects of the same unified consciousness. In the life-game, man fulfils himself in the Supreme by realising that God is man's own highest self. The Supreme reveals Himself through man, who serves as His instrument for world transformation and perfection.

Sri Chinmoy does not charge a fee for his spiritual guidance, nor does he charge for his frequent concerts or public meditations. His only fee, he says, is the seeker's sincere inner cry. He takes a personal interest in each of his students, and when he accepts a disciple, he takes full responsibility for that seeker's inner progress. In New York, Sri Chinmoy meditates in person with his disciples several times a week and offers regular meditation sessions for the general public. Students living outside New York see Sri Chinmoy during worldwide gatherings that take place three times a year, during visits to New York, or during the Master's frequent trips to their cities. They find that the inner bond between Master and disciple transcends physical separation.

Sri Chinmoy accepts students at all levels of development, from beginners to advanced seekers, and lovingly guides them inwardly and outwardly according to their individual needs.

Sri Chinmoy personally leads an active life, demonstrating most vividly that spirituality is not an escape from the world, but a means of transforming it. He has written more than 1,100 books, which include plays, poems, stories, essays, commentaries and answers to questions on spirituality. He has painted thousands of widely exhibited mystical paintings and composed thousands of devotional songs. Performing his own compositions on a wide variety of instruments, he has offered a series of several hundred Peace Concerts in cities around the world.

A naturally gifted athlete and a firm believer in the spiritual benefits of physical fitness, Sri Chinmoy encourages his disciples to participate in sports. Under his inspirational guidance, the international Sri Chinmoy Marathon Team organises hundreds of road races, including the longest certified race in the world (3,100) miles, and biannually stages a global relay run for peace.

Sri Chinmoy's achievements as a weight lifter have also earned him considerable renown. To demonstrate that inner peace gained through meditation can be a tangible source of outer strength, he has lifted objects weighing as much as 7,000 pounds. In addition, he has honored more than 1,700 individuals by physically lifting them overhead on a specially constructed platform in an awards programme entitled "Lifting Up the World with a Oneness-Heart."

ADDITIONAL TITLES
by *Sri Chinmoy*

GOD is...
Selected Writings of Sri Chinmoy

This long awaited book gathers Sri Chinmoy's insights about God into one volume. These selections are drawn from the more than one thousand books he has written in over thirty years of teaching spirituality and meditation. His intimate knowledge of God transcends religious dogma and scripture, shedding light on all seekers' paths to God. The simplicity of the language belies an astonishing depth of knowledge that goes beyond the intellect and directly communicates the wisdom of the soul.

Topics include: Can the exixtence of God be proven? • The cause of your separation from God • Should you ever fear God? • Seeing God in all • The meaning of suffering • Increasing your need for God • How to know what God wants you to do with your life. $12.95

The Three Branches of India's Life-Tree: Commentaries on the Vedas, the Upanishads and the Bhagavad Gita

This book brings together in one volume Sri Chinmoy's commentaries on three ancient Indian scriptures which are the foundations of Hindu spiritual tradition. His approach is clear and practical, and at the same time profound and richly poetic. In a style unmistakably his own, Sri Chinmoy makes direct and personal contact with the reader, who joins him on a journey through the wisdom of these celebrated classics. This book is both an excellent introduction for readers who are coming to the subject for the first time, and a series of illumining meditations for those who already know it well. $13.95

Meditation: Man-Perfection in God-Satisfaction

Presented with the simplicity and clarity that have become the hallmark of Sri Chinmoy's writings, this book is easily one of the most comprehensive guides to meditation available.

Topics include: Proven meditation techniques that anyone can learn • How to still the restless mind • Developing the power of concentration • Carrying peace with you always • Awakening the heart centre to discover the power of your soul • The significance of prayer. Plus a special section in which Sri Chinmoy answers questions on a wide range of experiences often encountered in meditation. $9.95

Beyond Within: A Philosophy for the Inner Life

"How can I carry on the responsibilities of life and still grow inwardly to find spiritual fulfilment?"

When your simple yearning to know the purpose of your life and feel the reality of God has you swimming against the tide, then the wisdom and guidance of a spiritual Master who has crossed these waters is priceless. Sri Chinmoy offers profound insight into man's relationship with God, and sound advice on how to integrate the highest spiritual aspirations into daily life.

Topics include: The transformation and perfection of the body • The spiritual journey • The relationship between the mind and physical illness • Using the soul's will to conquer life's problems • Overcoming fear of failure • The purpose of pain and suffering • Becoming conscious of your own divine nature. $13.95

Kundalini: The Mother-Power

En route to his own spiritual realisation, Sri Chinmoy attained mastery over the Kundalini and occult powers. In this book he explains techniques for awakening the Kundalini and the chakras. He warns of the dangers and pitfalls to be avoided and discusses some of the occult powers that come with the opening of the chakras.

Topics include: The Mother aspect of the Divine • Concentration techniques to awaken the Kundalini • Kundalini and Hatha Yoga • Mantras and the opening of the chakras • Opening the third eye • Sexuality and occult power • The different approaches to Kundalini Yoga including Tantric and Vedantic. $7.95

Yoga and the Spiritual Life

Yoga means union—union with God. Each person's journey in life begins and ultimately ends with that union. Written in a practical vein, this book offers the newcomer, as well as the advanced seeker, a deep understanding of the theories, methods and inner realities of the philosophy of Yoga and Eastern mysticism.

Of particular interest is the section devoted to questions and answers on the soul and the inner life. As an illumined Yogi who has experienced these realities firsthand, Sri Chinmoy's answers offer a clarity and authenticity rarely encountered.

Topics include: What is Yoga? • Who is fit for Yoga? • Meditation • The Law of Karma • Reincarnation and the soul's evolution • Morality and sin, $8.95

The Summits of God-Life: Samadhi and Siddhi
A genuine account of the world beyond time and space

An authoritative discussion of consciousness and the very advanced stages of spiritual practice. Few people in history have attained these highest states and fewer still have clearly revealed their meanings and import in such a simple and understandable language. In fact, as Sri Chinmoy explains, the very use of language is totally inadequate to convey the qualities of these ineffable realms—making this book a rare treasure.

Topics include: Infinity • Planes of consciousness • Nirvana • Trance states • Liberation and realisation • Ananda (bliss) and more. $6.95

Inner and Outer Peace

A powerful yet simple approach for establishing peace in your own life and the world.

Sri Chinmoy speaks of the higher truths that energise the quest for world peace, giving contemporary expression to the relationship between our personal search for inner peace and the world's search for outer peace. He reveals truths which lift the peace of the world above purely political and historical considerations, contributing his spiritual understanding and inspiration to the cause of world peace. $7.95

A Child's Heart and a Child's Dreams
Growing Up with Spiritual Wisdom—A Guide for Parents and Children

Sri Chinmoy offers practical advice on a subject that is not only an idealist's dream but every concerned parent's lifeline: fostering your child's spiritual life, watching him or her grow up with a love of God and a heart of self-giving.

Topics include: Ensuring your child's spiritual growth • Education and spirituality—their meeting ground • Answers to children's questions about God • A simple guide to meditation and a special section of children's stories guaranteed to delight and inspire. $7.95

The Master and the Disciple

What is a Guru? There are running gurus, diet gurus and even stock market gurus. But to those in search of spiritual enlightenment, the Guru is not merely an 'expert'; he is the way to their self-realisation. Sri Chinmoy says in this definitive book on the Guru-disciple relationship: "The most important thing a Guru does for his spiritual children is to make them aware of something vast and infinite within themselves, which is nothing other than God Himself."

Topics include: How to find a Guru • Telling a real spiritual Master from a false one • How to recognise your own Guru • Making the most spiritual progress while under the guidance of a spiritual Master • What it means when a Guru takes on your *karma* • Plus a special section of stories and plays illustrating the more subtle aspects of the subject. $7.95

Everest-Aspiration

Everest represents the highest height, and at the same time humanity's determination to attain that height. The spiritual Everest is union with the Creator, and through the ages humanity has aspired poignantly toward this loftiest goal.

The ascent to Everest's peak is arduous, but an expert guide can reveal the way toward the crowning fulfilment. On these pages Sri Chinmoy speaks with the voice of both a God-seeker and God-knower, leading the aspiring reader's heart ever higher toward the summit of self-knowledge, the zenith of God-oneness. $8.95

Siddhartha Becomes the Buddha

The light of the Buddha has shone as a beacon, calling men from across the sea of darkness. Like lost children, millions of seekers have reached out to the light and the Buddha has shown them the Way.

Who exactly was the Buddha? In these ten plays, adapted from different incidents in the Buddha's life, spiritual Master Sri Chinmoy answers this question from the deepest spiritual point of view. The poetry and power of the Buddha's message take on a new, real and inner beauty as conveyed through the dramatic medium of these short plays. $5.95

The Silent Teaching

In this concise and inspiring introduction to meditation and the inner life, Sri Chinmoy exhorts the seeker in us: "Here on earth, in the hustle and bustle of life, we have to practice spirituality...Here on earth we have to realise the Highest."

To that end, this book gives the beginner the basics in the theory, vision and practice of meditation. $4.95

On Wings of Silver Dreams

With their prophetic messages, dreams can offer us deep inner wisdom. They may foretell the future, reveal the solution to a problem or give us a spiritual experience. We are healed by dreaming of a beloved friend or family member.

But there is also the darker side of dreams. Frightening nightmares destroy our sleep. We find ourselves in menacing worlds unable to cry out for help. How can we decipher dreams that come to us?

This collection of Sri Chinmoy's answers to questions on dreams guides us through the confusing labyrinth, teaching us to understand the significance of some common dreams, and to gain some control over the kinds of dreams we have. $6.95

Peace-Blossom-Fragrance
Aphorisms on Peace

Dedicated to the United Nations on its 50th anniversary and to peace-lovers everywhere, this special book is beautifully inspiring. Each page is a field of serene blue sky and wispy clouds bordered by Sri Chinmoy's own charming bird drawings. The 700 aphorisms on peace offer a profound and illumining look at the divine nature of peace, its relationship to humanity's age-old quest and secrets of its attainment. Anyone seeking peace in their own life or praying for world peace will find this book to be a revelation as well as a delight.

$7.95

MUSIC OF SRI CHINMOY

Flute Music for Meditation

While in a state of deep meditation Sri Chinmoy plays his haunting melodies on the electric echo-flute. Its rich and soothing tones will transport you to the highest realms of inner peace and harmony.

Cassette $9.95 CD $12.95

Inner and Outer Peace

A tapestry of music, poetry and aphorisms on inner and outer peace. Sri Chinmoy's profoundly inspiring messages are woven into a calm and uplifting musical composition with the Master singing, chanting and playing the flute, harmonium, esraj, cello, harpsichord and synthesizer.

Cassette $9.95

Ecstasy's Trance: *Esraj Music for Meditation*

The esraj, often described as a soothing combination of sitar and violin, is Sri Chinmoy's favourite instrument. With haunting intensity, he seems to draw the music from another dimension. The source of these compositions is the silent realm of the deepest and most sublime meditation. Listen to the music and enter this realm, a threshold rarely crossed in the course of one's lifetime.

Cassette $9.95

The Dance of Light:
Sri Chinmoy Plays the Flute

Forty-seven soft and gentle flute melodies that will carry you directly to the source of joy and beauty: your own aspiring heart. Be prepared to float deep, deep within on waves of music that "come from Heaven itself."

Cassette $9.95

To order books or tapes, request a catalogue, or find out more about Sri Chinmoy or the Sri Chinmoy Centres worldwide, please write to:

Aum Publications
86-24 Parsons Blvd.
Jamaica, NY 11432

When ordering a book or cassette, send check or money order made out to Aum Publications. Please add $3.50 postage for the first book ($2.00 for cassette) and 75¢ for each additional item. Prices valid thru January 1999. Please inquire about sales outside the United States and Canada.